THE ELUSIVE CITY

The
Elusive City

Five Centuries of Design, Ambition and Miscalculation

JONATHAN BARNETT

Icon Editions

1817
HARPER & ROW, PUBLISHERS, New York
Cambridge, Philadelphia, San Francisco, London
Mexico City, São Paulo, Singapore, Sydney

The preliminary research for this book was supported by a grant from the Design Arts Program of the National Endowment for the Arts.

FIRST EDITION

Designer: Jénine Holmes

Library of Congress Cataloging-in-Publication Data

Barnett, Jonathan.   The elusive city.

  (Icon editions)
  Includes index.
  1. City planning—History. 2. Architecture, Modern—History. 3. Architecture and society. I. Title. NA9094.B37   1986   711'.4'09   85-45176L
ISBN 0-06-430377-2   86 87 88 89 90 HAL 10 9 8 7 6 5 4 3 2 1
ISBN 0-06-430155-9 (pbk.)   88 89 90 HAL 10 9 8 7 6 5 4 3 2

To my wife, Nory Miller, the architectural critic and editor, with great appreciation for her invaluable critical and editorial suggestions

Contents

THE ELUSIVE CITY

1
Preindustrial Traditions

There has been a long struggle in western civilization between attempts to design cities and the relatively intractable social and economic forces that make city design so difficult to achieve. While some city designs have been based on utopian expectations of social transformation, many were conceived as practicable remedies to urban problems of their day, were at least partially carried out and continue to be influential. City-design concepts have often been applied in entirely different economic, political and personal circumstances from those in which they originated, frequently with far-from-expected results. In some ways city design seems to have followed the same path as military technology, where the generals are always prepared to fight the previous war. An understanding of city design thus requires both a chronological account and a detailed exploration of the major design ideas that have entered the history of cities sequentially but continued simultaneously, producing both intricate interrelationships and unsettling juxtapositions.

The complexities of this subject are often lost in the divisions among scholarly disciplines or fall between the boundaries of different professions. Art historians tend to look at the work of individual artists or specific historical periods, and more often discuss buildings as isolated artifacts than as parts of cities. Urban historians give far less attention to the physical fabric of cities than they do to political events and social and economic patterns. Practitioners of architecture and other design professions have often looked to history only for the justification of a specific polemic or as a prelude to descriptions of their own work. City planning, as a relatively new profession, has sought to distance itself from architecture and landscape architecture, both to create a separate identity and for fear of appearing frivolous in the eyes of city officials by being overly concerned with aesthetic matters.

Before the industrial revolution there were many similarities among cities from widely divergent cultures and historical periods. Successful cities almost always grew up on rivers and harbors, because large quantities of goods were moved most effectively by water. The demands of defense required walls; the costliness of fortifications gave cities a compact shape. A circular wall system enclosed the largest amount of town for a given amount of stone or brick, a fact that was more important to cities run by citizens who had to raise the money among themselves than to cities built by military commanders or emperors. Within the walls there was usually a citadel, a last resort if the outer defenses failed.

Inside a city, the major thoroughfares were likely to lead from the necessarily limited number of gates to a central market square, where the important religious and public buildings were often located. The main streets subdivided the city into neighborhoods, crossed by smaller lanes, including functional districts that would serve the whole city, such as a street of armorers or a warehouse district by the waterfront.

A specialist may have been employed to design the fortifications or important buildings, but for much of history there was no concept that anyone should seek to design the city itself. Many cities evolved gradually from villages, their growth spurred by an especially good location, energetic leadership or abundant resources.

By contrast, preconceived designs were likely to be imposed when cities were rebuilt after a war or when new cities were founded as colonies or military outposts.

Grids were the most common device in such circumstances. The concept of dividing a city into square or rectangular blocks with long, straight streets is often attributed to Hippodamus of Miletus, who, according to Aristotle's *Politics* and other references in classical literature, designed the Greek colony of Thurii in southern Italy and redesigned Piraeus, the harbor city of Athens, during the age of Pericles. Hippodamus probably brought the grid plan to Greece but was unlikely to have been its inventor. His own home town of Miletus, on the Asian mainland in what is now Turkey, was destroyed by the Persians and rebuilt on a right-angle plan after the Persians were expelled in 479 B.C., when Hippodamus is generally thought to have been either a child or a very young man. In fact, grid plans had been in use in the Ionian cities of Asia Minor since the seventh century B.C. and have been used in many other cultures, including Babylon, China and India, without there being any demonstrated link among them.

Planned Roman cities were based on the pattern of the Roman military camp, typically a walled square or rectangle divided by two main, straight streets crossing at right angles, with other streets parallel to them to form a rectangular grid, and a central forum near the major intersection. Pompeii had a plan of this kind, as did the Roman cities on the sites of Florence and Turin.

Vitruvius, the Roman architect of the early imperial period who wrote the only text on architecture to survive from Greece or Rome (although we know from Vitruvius's own internal references that his was one of many), includes a few short chapters on the layout and most healthful orientation of city streets in his *Ten Books on Architecture*. His words have been pored over, interpreted and reinterpreted. The scholarly clerics who laid out New Haven, Connecticut, in 1638 assumed that streets should be at right angles to each other and interpreted Vitruvius's prescriptions as a design for a city made up of nine equal squares. In Italy, Renaissance theorists read the same chapter as describing a polygonal city with eight major avenues radiating from a central point, the basis for many drawings of ideal city plans.

A few new communities were constructed during the Renaissance in accordance with such polygonal plans, with their star-shaped pattern of surrounding ramparts. The rampart pattern itself, a response to the invention of cannons, was imposed on many existing cities from the fifteenth through the eighteenth centuries.

More important for the future development of cities, however, were concepts of architectural space that derive originally from Renaissance painting and theater design and begin to find actual expression in cities during the 1500s. The relationship between buildings and nature was redefined, with the building first dominating nature and then, as an alternative, blended into the natural environment. The concept of the spectator's viewpoint, either static or moving, also provided alternative ways of thinking about buildings and their surroundings. These ideas lead to the first city designs in the modern sense of the term, and it is with them that this book begins.

To understand the subsequent history of city design is to understand much of what has created the contemporary city and much of what is happening to it now, as designers rediscover concepts long thought to be outmoded and attempt to combine them with the tall building, modern technology and the exigencies of late-twentieth-century life.

2

The Monumental City

Early on Sunday morning, September 2, 1666, a fire broke out in the city of London which, by the time it was put out late the following Tuesday night, had destroyed 433 acres, almost the whole of the city.

Christopher Wren was at that time a thirty-four-year-old professor of astronomy at Oxford and had only recently begun to design buildings. However, he already held a position that put him in line to be the head of the Royal Office of Works, and his designs for the reconstruction of London's old St. Paul's cathedral had been approved just six days before the fire.

On September 11, 1666, barely a week after the fire was out, Wren presented a plan for rebuilding London to King Charles II and his council. Wren proposed to use the reconstruction of London as a means to give the city a completely new street plan. He was so eager to seize this opportunity that he not only made preliminary surveys for the new streets in a week, but had done the work while the ruins were still almost too hot to walk on and were filled with dangerous piles of debris and hidden cavities that had once been cellars.

London before the fire had resembled most other cities of its day. It had a wall and a citadel, the Tower of London; and a cathedral, St. Paul's; and its winding streets outlined a pattern of small precincts, each with its own parish church. The arrangement of the city was the product of a slow evolutionary development on the site that the Romans had made their provincial capital, Londinium.

European cities of the time had grown and changed as slowly as London. A German architect, Karl Gruber, prepared an unusual set of drawings for *Ein Deutsche Stadt,* published in 1914, which describes the evolution of a hypothetical German city from the twelfth century to the eighteenth. While Gruber was open to the criticism that he was creating fictional documents, his drawings clarify similarities of city development that are often lost in the specifics of local history.

In 1180 Gruber's city has a moat and a wall, winding streets of steeply gabled houses, a citadel, and the cathedral facing the town hall across the market square. There is some development outside the walls, notably a monastery on the near side of the river. By 1350 the city has grown, the near bank of the river has been fortified and has its own streets of gabled houses, and a small suburban precinct has grown up across the moat, but otherwise 170 years have not seen radical change. By 1580 the fortifications of the city have been improved as a result of the introduction of gunpowder, and some primitive cannons can be seen on the battlements. The cathedral and the castle have been rebuilt, but it is recognizably the same city two and a half centuries later and not that much different from the city in the first drawing, four centuries before.

London did have some significant differences from European cities of the type shown in Gruber's drawings. At the time of the fire London had grown extensively beyond its walls and relied on the navy for its defense from foreign invaders, a policy vindicated by the defeat of the Spanish Armada in 1588. Also, unlike comparable cities across the Channel, London had no central market square. Instead, a main street, Cheapside, was the place where other major streets intersected, and shops and markets were strung out along this network. In most ways, however, London in 1666 was a typical medieval city; it looked the way almost everyone at the time assumed cities were supposed to look. Wren's proposal that such a city could be entirely replanned, even after a disastrous fire, was a startlingly new idea.

Wren was a scholar and scientist before he became an architect. He learned the essentials of architecture from books. The transmission of architectural ideas through printed books and engraved drawings and maps was gradually to displace the medieval system in which architectural ideas were transmitted from master to apprentice and followed the movement of architects and master craftsmen from one building site to the next. The invention of printing made it possible for a designer to assimilate and use an entirely new mode of architectural expression, so that English architecture in the seventeenth century, under the influence of scholarly architects like Inigo Jones and Christopher Wren, went straight from buildings that were close to the late medieval tradition to architecture that was comparable to Baroque work being done in Italy and France at the same time. Scholarship had also made familiar buildings from the beginning of the Renaissance onward, enabling Jones and Wren to select their favorite elements from any point in the pattern of historical development.

Many commentators seem to consider Wren's plan for London to be a relatively unimportant interlude in a career that was to lead Wren to be the architect of the new St. Paul's, to design or supervise the design of all the new churches built to replace those lost in the fire, and to be the architect for many other important buildings. But Wren's plan, had it been carried out, might have changed the history of city design. It was as radical a departure from the existing English city as Renaissance architecture from Tudor or Gothic buildings. Wren was careful to make the new streets link up to the old wherever buildings stood undamaged, but instead of the old winding streets, he proposed two new straight avenues starting in a triangular plaza in front of a rebuilt St. Paul's and leading directly across the walled city, one to Aldgate and the other to the Tower. A third avenue would start at Newgate, on the western side of the city, and meet the avenue to Aldgate at a large oval plaza that would be the setting for a new Royal Exchange. Around this plaza would be all the other financial institutions—the mint, the excise office, the hall of the Goldsmith's Company and so on.

The entire north frontage of the Thames across the burned area was to be treated in a new formalized manner. At the entrance to London Bridge, Wren proposed a semicircular plaza with straight avenues fanning out from it. Two of these new streets would lead to small circular plazas along the main avenues from St. Paul's to the Tower, and other straight streets would radiate from them. A third circular plaza with straight streets radiating from it was planned for the burned area to the west of the city walls. The district around St. Paul's, between the two sets of radial streets, was treated as a series of almost rectangular blocks, their angles adjusted somewhat to fit into the overall scheme.

The king was sufficiently impressed by Wren's plan, and by plans put forward a little later by John Evelyn and others, to decree that no rebuilding should begin in the city until an overall reconstruction scheme had been drawn up and approved. London's business leaders were concerned, however, that Wren's plan would require such a complex realignment of properties that recovery from the fire would be prevented far longer than if everyone could simply rebuild on the old foundations. Wren's plan also required rebuilding parish churches on new sites, a disturbing concept because people thought of city geography in terms of the parishes. Charles II, who had been back on his throne for only six years, was necessarily sensitive to the limits of his authority. Moreover, the country was in the midst of a war with the Dutch and the French (this was the war in which the British seized New Amsterdam from the Dutch in 1666 and renamed it New York), and there was no money to spare to subsidize urban redevelopment.

The king created a committee of six to draft the standards for rebuilding. He appointed three of the members, including Wren, and he let the city merchants choose the others. The committee first tried to get all property owners in the burned part of London to submit an accurate survey of their land, a necessary precondition for the exchange of property to implement a new street system. When only 10 percent of the owners complied, and it became clear that the king was not going to provide an alternative by paying for a complete survey, the committee was forced to plan the reconstruction of London on the old pattern, with some wider streets and new standards for more fireproof buildings.

The long vistas and geometric plazas that Wren tried to introduce into London had a long and complex history. The ability to think about cities as a series of connected spaces linked by vistas seems to be related to the rediscovery of perspective by Italian artists in the early fifteenth century. The ideal cities that formed the background for painted scenes were translated first into stage scenery, then into garden design, and later into actual city squares and streets, and as this evolution took place, concepts of space also evolved from individual squares surrounded by buildings to sequences of spaces linked by avenues.

The first comprehensive replanning of a city according to these new pictorial principles was carried out in Rome by Pope Sixtus V and his architect, Domenico Fontana, between 1585 and 1590. Sixtus was sixty-four when he was elected pope, and had pretended to ill health to make himself a more acceptable compromise candidate who could not be expected to live too long. But the threat of death was all too real, and Sixtus V's pontificate was a headlong rush to accomplish as much as possible before the inevitable. Sixtus V turned out to have five years and four months before he died of malaria at the age of sixty-nine, which makes his replanning of Rome all the more remarkable: he compressed into five years work that might ordinarily have been expected to take twenty years or more.

Sixtus V also reformed the structure of the papacy to increase its revenue and stabilize its finances, creating the resources for his great public works and still leaving the papal treasury in far better shape than he found it; he was immersed, too, in ecclesiastical, political and military problems. In such an active reign it is unlikely that he would have had the time to plan the urban development that he set in motion from the first day he was in power. It is probable that Sixtus and Fontana had their designs in readiness, in the hope that the campaign for the papacy would be successful.

There would have been plenty of time to work out these plans. During the whole thirteen-year reign of Pope Gregory XIII, Sixtus, then Cardinal Montalto, had been out of favor. In 1581 he had bought a hilltop site near Santa Maria Maggiore; and Domenico Fontana designed for him a relatively modest country villa, with gardens laid out in perspective vistas between avenues of trees and garden walls in what had become the established mode of Italian garden design. It was in this villa that the plans to remake Rome were probably drawn.

Of course, Sixtus V was not the first pope to undertake changes in the city of Rome, and he took care to incorporate earlier designs into his overall scheme. One of the most important of these predecessor designs was the rebuilding of the plaza at the city end of the bridge that connects Rome with its citadel, Castel Sant' Angelo. The streets leading out of this plaza were regularized into a radiating pattern during the reign of Pope Paul III (1534–1549). The design of the plaza is related to Baroque concepts of stage scenery such as the permanent set designed by Palladio's pupil Vincenzo Scamozzi for Palladio's Teatro Olimpico in Vicenza, which is perhaps the most famous example of its kind. It shows, through a central arch and two side doors, glimpses of seven streets lined with buildings whose uniform cornice lines vanish in an exaggerated perspective. The theater was completed in 1585, the same year that Sixtus began the transformation of Rome.

The key element of Sixtus V's plan for Rome was a succession of long, straight streets, the changes of direction marked by piazzas with central obelisks. The streets linked the major pilgrimage destinations through sections of Rome that had been essentially uninhabited for centuries. (Sixtus and Fontana also planned and built a new aqueduct which restored water service to the districts that the new streets opened up to habitation.)

The construction by Sixtus V of the Piazza del Popolo at the entrance to Rome was intended to make that plaza into a theater that enjoyed vistas down the streets that fanned out from it like the glimpses of city streets at the Teatro Olimpico, although the concept of the piazza was not fully realized until the nineteenth century.

The uniform streetscape evoked by the Teatro Olimpico was also implied by the long, straight streets of Sixtus's Rome, although these streets, constructed mainly through underpopulated or abandoned parts of the city, had no buildings along much of their length for many years. Uniform street architecture was not an essential element of earlier Renaissance concepts of architectural space. Sebastiano Serlio's often published sequence of theater sets, from his architectural textbook, *L'Architettura*, shows an ideal streetscape of Renaissance buildings as a suitable backdrop for tragedy, a more realistic mixture of medieval and Renaissance structures as a setting for comedy, and a landscape vista as the satyric scene. Even in the tragic street scene, the buildings are by no means uniform, reflecting the individuality of buildings in most ideal cities painted during the "high" Renaissance.

Michelangelo's design for the Capitol at Rome, begun in 1536, is an important step in creating the apparatus that other designers would extend into planning principles, including the concept of giving architectural uniformity to external space. The placement of the two flanking buildings to create an exaggerated perspective, the architectural vocabulary of colonnade and colossal order, the organization of the pavement pattern around a central sculpture, all were to prove extremely influential. Giorgio Vasari's later design for the courtyard of the Uffizi Palace in Florence, with its buildings canted to produce an exaggerated perspective and its uniform cornices and moldings, may have been a direct influence on the set design of the Teatro Olimpico.

Lewis Mumford has suggested that the long, straight street and the concept of uniform, repetitive facades may have been a response to the introduction of horse-drawn carriages into cities, which begins at about this time. A pedestrian or an individual on horseback can negotiate a more complicated street pattern and has time for a more idiosyncratic perception of a city than a passenger peering from the window of a swiftly moving coach.

Uniformity of spatial enclosure, so hard to obtain with buildings, could be realized much more easily in garden design. Long vistas, extending the architectural system of a great house, could be enclosed by walls and plantations of trees and enlivened by pools, fountains and cascades.

The rondel, or rond-point, was originally created as a setting for the ceremonial hunts that took place at court. The royal personage and his entourage waited on horseback in the center of the circular forest clearing with radiating avenues leading out of it. Beaters worked through the woods to flush a stag out of hiding. When the stag crossed an avenue, the hunt came dashing down the clearing after it.

The circular opening designed by André Le Nôtre for the forest at the end of the long axis on the garden side of Versailles, with radiating avenues leading from it, turned the rondel into an ornamental device for dealing with the intersections of long axial vistas. In addition to the long, straight garden avenues enclosed by plantations of trees on the garden side of Versailles, the side of the palace that faces the town forms a forecourt where three avenues converge in a fan-shaped pattern that is similar to the streets originating at the Piazza del Popolo.

Le Nôtre, the son of a royal landscape gardener, was trained in both landscape design and architecture, and was able to bring to his first important commission, the park at Vaux-le-Vicomte for the royal finance minister, Nicolas Fouquet, a way of using landscape in an architectural manner which was to create an integral relationship between the park and the chateau, by Louis Le Vau, that went beyond the axis and terraces of Italian garden design. The splendor of Vaux attracted the attention of the young Louis XIV for two reasons: first, as an assertion of power over nature, the park at Vaux was far more royal than any of the king's own palaces; second, where had the finance minister found the money to support his regal pretensions? After an investigation, Fouquet was imprisoned for the rest of his life, and Le Nôtre was put to work turning the park of the king's hunting lodge at Versailles into something more splendid than Vaux-le-Vicomte, while the architect Louis Le Vau and, later, Jules Hardouin Mansart, designed the elaborate palace.

The gardens at Versailles can be seen as a kind of city plan, because they represented a controlled environment for the centralized power of the court. The rond-points and radiating avenues at Versailles were added to the apparatus of plaza and vista already created in Rome to become a vocabulary of city design in Wren's plan for London.

Roman plazas with radiating streets appear in Wren's plan at the two most important entrances to the city: the foot of London Bridge and the top of Ludgate Hill in front of the newly positioned St. Paul's, a gateway to the walled city that is a close analogue to the entrance to Rome at the Piazza del Popolo. The way St. Paul's is placed at the origin of two major avenues would seem to show that Wren was familiar not only with the map of Sixtus V's Rome but also with the way Carlo Rainaldi's twin churches, begun in 1662, frame the streets entering the Piazza del Popolo.

There is no evidence that Wren ever journeyed to Rome, but he did make a long visit to France in 1665. The development of the gardens at Versailles actually did not begin until the year after Wren made his plan for London and two years after his visit to France, but Wren may well have seen Le Nôtre's plans while they were in preparation, and he would have known Le Nôtre's modifications to the Tuileries gardens and the design of Vaux-le-Vicomte, where analogous motifs are employed.

Wren, a royalist from a prominent royalist family, was attracted to design ideas employed by autocrats. But Sixtus V, the absolute ruler of the Papal States as well as pope, confined most of his town-planning efforts to parts of Rome that were essentially uninhabited. Louis XIV asserted his symbolic primacy over France through the long vistas of the gardens at suburban Versailles, but he left Paris itself relatively unchanged.

If Wren's plan had been adopted, it would have had a far stronger effect on an actual city than the works of Louis XIV and Sixtus V. However, the merchants of the city of London owed their allegiance to their own businesses and trade associations. There was little reason for them to be sympathetic to design concepts that would give grandeur to London itself, when implementation of these designs might prolong the rebuilding process and endanger their economic recovery. Wren did provide many rectangular blocks, an ancient device but something of an innovation in England at the time, which had the advantage of permitting incremental development; but he placed little emphasis on another Renaissance city planning device, which had already become established in London's mercantile society—the city square surrounded by individual row houses linked by uniform facades.

Robert Hooke, who as city surveyor was the employee of the London mercantile establishment and had been appointed by the merchants to the post-fire reconstruction committee, had attempted an alternative to Wren's plan, based on city squares and a rectangular street grid. This plan also required a new survey and did not succeed, but the square had a good claim to be the appropriate expression of bourgeois society, based as it was on a grouping of individual houses, joined to form a more palatial whole. In 1631, during the reign of Charles I, Inigo Jones, then the head of the Royal Office of Works, had drawn the plans of such a square for the subdivision of land at Covent Garden belonging to the Earl of Bedford. According to documentary research carried out by John Summerson, there is evidence that the earl received royal permission to subdivide, at a time when there were strong restrictions on new house construction, by making a payment of £2,000 and agreeing to use Jones as the master planner for the development. Jones had been to Italy and had seen Italian city squares like the one at Leghorn. He would also have been familiar with patterns of streets and squares in ideal city designs, such as the city in Vincenzo Scamozzi's *L'Idea della Architettura Universale.* Jones actually met Scamozzi during a trip to Italy in 1614. Jones was also familiar with French examples like the Place Ducale in Charleville and the Place Royale (now the Place des Vosges) in Paris, which were closer to his immediate requirements, and he knew the large number of English palaces and colleges grouped around courtyards.

Jones's design created rows of houses on the north and east sides of the square, with arcades along the ground floor. Regularly spaced pilasters were aligned with the piers supporting the ground-floor arches, giving the upper two floors a regular, repeating rhythm. The roofs were continuous and the spacing of the attic windows regular, unlike the Place Royale or Charleville, where the separate nature of the constituent houses was expressed by hipped roofs. The west side of the square centered on a church designed by Inigo Jones, which was surrounded by more modest houses that were also part of the plan. The south side of the square was originally the garden fence of the Earl of Bedford's own house. The decision to build a church reflected the precinctual nature of London at that time; a parish church was necessary to give a neighborhood an identity.

Covent Garden, and the less formal arrangement of Lincoln's Inn Fields, where Jones had at least some supervisory role, were models of a more incremental form of urban organization than the great avenue. The westward expansion of London, which accelerated as a result of the fire, was to make much use of the square, but relationships from square to square are informal, even ad hoc, dictated by the property lines of the estates that were being subdivided.

Up until the mid-eighteenth century, the city square seems to have been understood essentially as an incident in the urban framework, a form of relief from the pattern of streets, rather than as a systematic ordering device in its own right. Squares were usually defined only as a site plan, as at Lincoln's Inn Fields, not as a fully developed architectural concept like Covent Garden.

The square did continue to be the chief design element of mercantile cities. Squares were used in the plan for Philadelphia that Thomas Holme laid out for William Penn in 1682. A public square marked the intersection of the two main streets in the center, and there was a square park or garden in each of the four quadrants.

Squares were used more systematically in the plan for Savannah of 1733 by James Oglethorpe, but still as a relief from the street grid. It was in the design of the new parts of Bath by John Wood and his son, also named John Wood, starting in 1727, that the row house–town square became in itself an instrument of coordinated city design.

Bath was a resort; houses were not occupied all year. Social distinctions in the architecture were blurred by the fact that few people felt they needed a really large house for a visit. On the other hand, almost everyone needed about the same number of entertaining spaces and bedrooms. Thus houses of similar size were available as building blocks for architectural compositions.

Despite their importance to the history of architecture and city planning, not much is known about the Woods. The detective work in piecing together the best available documentary evidence has again been done by John Summerson. John Wood senior seems to have practiced as both a landscape architect and an architect at a very early age: if the date of birth given in his obituaries is to be believed, while still a teen-ager. He was involved for several years in the development of the West End of London, both as a designer and as a speculative builder. The development pattern in London since Covent Garden had been for a master plan to be drawn for a square or street, and for individual builder-developers to undertake the construction of a relatively small number of houses—one side of a square, for example. Sometimes the developer was the owner of the property, but the property owners seldom attempted to be the developers for all of their land. The capitalization and the risk were thus divided among several entrepreneurs, a pattern that continues to exist in subdivision development today.

John Summerson calls attention to the design by Edward Shepherd for part of one frontage of Grosvenor Square in London, dating from the mid-1720s. Instead of each house being a similar, repeating unit, in the way that Inigo Jones had designed Covent Garden, and instead of a random pattern of different groups of houses, which had become the London norm, Shepherd took a row of individual houses and treated it as if it were a single palatial building with a central colonnade and pediment. The concept was not a completely successful design because Shepherd did not control the full frontage of the Square, but Summerson argues persuasively that here is the germ of the idea that the Woods were to develop so successfully in Bath and that was to influence so many other architects.

Wood had evidently realized that Bath was on the verge of a major development boom and actively sought to become its architect. From the beginning he also seems to have had a concept that Bath, once the site of a Roman city, should have Roman features like a forum and a circus.

The site planning for the houses that John Wood built at Bath from 1727 to the 1750s followed the pattern already established in London: a street and a square. At Queen Square, however, Wood was able to build a row of eight houses unified behind a single palatial facade with central pediment and end pavilions, showing that he was thinking in terms of a three-dimensional architectural realization, and not just following a typical site plan. The Circus, which was begun just before John Wood senior's death in 1754, is a complete architectural concept and something almost unprecedented in the history of city design.

The Circus at Bath is a group of thirty-three houses arranged in a circle at the intersection of three streets. In plan it is similar to the rond-points familiar from garden design, to Mansart's Place des Victoires in Paris, and to several unexecuted circular plazas that appear on Pierre Patte's composite map of Paris published in 1765, and not unlike the circular plazas Wren showed in his London plan. However, it was not clear what kind of architecture Wren imagined for his circular plazas. The Woods chose a simple, uniform three-story elevation with engaged columns. The columns are Doric on the ground floor, then Ionic above and Corinthian at the top story, an allusion to the Colosseum in Rome, which employs this architectural sequence on its exterior.

John Wood's classical learning seems to have been impressionistic at best. The Circus Maximus at Rome is an elongated oval, not a circle; the Colosseum is elliptical. Perhaps Wood didn't care that he was nowhere close to the Roman originals he cites; certainly what matters to us is the quality of the result.

John Wood the younger completed an even more interesting and influential group of houses off a street that leads away from the Circus: the Royal Crescent. Here a much clearer architectural elevation of basement and two-story columns produces a strongly modeled and unified building. On the site, the reason for the amphitheater shape for this group of houses is immediately apparent, as the topography permits each house to enjoy a spectacular view.

The Woods' circus and crescent became the middle-class equivalent to the royal avenue and vista, a means of designing cities that was in keeping with a free-market economy and did not require the control of an autocrat. Circus and crescent were to be widely influential for the rest of the eighteenth century and most of the nineteenth, notably at English seaside resorts, in the West End of London and in the new part of Edinburgh, where a succession of circuses and crescents were added in the early nineteenth century to James Craig's 1767 design, which has squares placed as formal ordering elements at each end of George Street.

On the Continent, where cities continued to be fortified, development was much less free than it was in England, and much investment went into the fortifications themselves. The last of Gruber's sequence of drawings depicting the development of a hypothetical German city shows its state in 1750. Although the basic plan of the medieval city remains, as well as the cathedral and many medieval houses, the quarter on the near side of the river has been rebuilt in Renaissance style, with symmetrical buildings, courtyards and a rectangular city square. Evidently the old mercantile social structure has been partially superseded by a society that creates large palaces. Even within the older portion of the city, Renaissance structures can be seen, as well as a Baroque parish church. The most startling change, however, is the star-shaped system of ramparts and moats, illustrative of the way most European cities had been fortified by the mid-seventeenth century. The regular geometry of the fortifications gave these cities a resemblance to the star-shaped diagrams of ideal cities that had been drawn by theorists since the fifteenth century.

Perhaps the most surprising combination of autocratic and mercantile city design in Europe during the eighteenth century was Karlsruhe, a provincial capital that was not considered important enough to be fortified. A palace, begun about 1715, was the center of a complete circle of radiating avenues. About two thirds of the avenues ran through garden and forest in the traditional manner, but the others became the streets of the town. However, as the town continued to develop, squares and streets of the mercantile city intersected with the autocrat's avenues, forming a series of awkward, unresolved angles.

A far more sophisticated synthesis of avenue and block, vista and square, was Major Pierre Charles L'Enfant's plan for Washington, D.C. L'Enfant came to America from France in 1777, when he was twenty-three, to enlist in Washington's army, offering his training as a military engineer. L'Enfant came from an artistic family; his father was a court painter and a member of the French Academy. After the Revolutionary War was over, L'Enfant settled in New York to practice architecture. George Washington, who had always gotten along well with the younger officer, selected L'Enfant to prepare the plans for the new capital city. Washington had played a major role in selecting the site for the city, and had himself negotiated the deal with the property owners that made the city possible: they would give up half of their land, plus whatever land was needed for the new streets and public buildings, in return for the added value that these streets and the new development would confer upon their remaining property. (Compensation was paid for land required for parks.) Washington met with L'Enfant on the site at the end of March 1791, and soon after sent him a letter enclosing his own ideas about the city. L'Enfant also received a sketch by Thomas Jefferson which set up a large-scale grid similar to the grids that would be planned for the newly acquired western territories when Jefferson was President. L'Enfant was clearly in a tricky situation. He was responsible to a group of commissioners, but was also receiving advice from the President, who had been trained as a surveyor, and from the Secretary of State, who was one of the great architectural intellects of the age.

L'Enfant's design abilities were equal to the challenge, but his political skills were not (he was still only thirty-seven). His letter to Washington explaining why Thomas Jefferson's grid plan would not be suitable was a model of tactlessness, describing regular grids as only suitable to level sites, "tiresome and insipid" and "wanting a sense of the really grand and truly beautiful." In his anxiety to secure the architectural commissions for the capitol and the President's house, L'Enfant opened himself to criticism by spending too much of his effort on preliminary architectural drawings. By the end of the year all his drawings had been confiscated by the commission (they have since been lost) and he had been dismissed, after trying to use his relationship to the President to evade the oversight of the commissioners.

Despite L'Enfant's personal failure, his design, taken out of his hands and drafted in final form by his associate, Andrew Ellicott, has been an enduring success. There is no direct documentary evidence of the sources that L'Enfant drew upon, but Elbert Peets, the city planner and city-design theorist, published an analysis in which he drew a genealogical table showing how L'Enfant's design derived from the Rome of Sixtus V, from Versailles and from plans for the reconstruction of London. Peets demonstrated how L'Enfant almost certainly used Versailles as a reference in organizing his plan's principal features. As his father was a court painter, L'Enfant had probably spent much of his childhood at Versailles and would have known the gardens better than any other model.

Respecting topography, as he had explained to Washington, L'Enfant placed the capitol on the highest piece of land, and the President's house at the only other elevated location. The triangle formed by the White House, the Capitol and the intersection of their two axes turns out to be almost exactly one and one half times the distance shown on Blondel's plan of Versailles between the Grand Trianon, the palace itself and the intersection of the two axes in the central basin of the canal. The width of L'Enfant's mall is almost exactly that of the canal at Versailles, while Pennsylvania Avenue is approximately the width of the Avenue de Trianon. Peets also shows how the shape of the square that L'Enfant planned to surround the President's house is derived from the two forecourts on the town side of the Palace of Versailles.

Peets also postulates that L'Enfant was heavily influenced by John Evelyn's third plan for the rebuilding of London. Evelyn, who served with Wren on the rebuilding committee, apparently kept tinkering with his plan in the hope that he could come up with a comprehensive reconstruction scheme that would be acceptable to the city merchants. In this final version, Evelyn found a way to keep most of the parish churches in their traditional locations, although he was still proposing a new street system.

While the resemblance of Washington to Evelyn's plan is undeniable, there is also a resemblance to Wren's London plan, which L'Enfant would equally probably have known, as the Evelyn and Wren plans were published together in the version that L'Enfant is most likely to have seen. L'Enfant might well have found Wren's design more architecturally sympathetic because of its greater emphasis on vistas and spaces. It is also, of course, perfectly possible that L'Enfant arrived at his design without reference to either London plan, as the logical result of trying to reconcile topography and dominant axes with a street grid that had strong political support as the most practical method of land subdivision.

L'Enfant may have alienated Thomas Jefferson with his tactlessness, but his eye for topography could have changed Jefferson's ideas about how to organize large architectural compositions. There is an anticipation of Jefferson's design for the University of Virginia in the way the axis from the Capitol goes straight along the open space of the Mall and across the river to the hills beyond, while the axis from the President's house is directed straight down the Potomac.

This axial relationship between clearly defined architectural space and unedited nature, which is also characteristic of the Royal Crescent at Bath, evidently did not appeal to Charles F. McKim, who at the turn of this century was to be instrumental in closing the University of Virginia's axis with a building and the Washington axes with the Lincoln Memorial and the Tidal Basin.

Jefferson accepted L'Enfant's plan and promoted its development, but his own continued preference for the grid can be seen in the mile-square pattern surveyed all over the western territories acquired during his administration. This grid in turn has had a pervasive effect on the cities and towns that have grown up in much of the United States, where the surveyor's square or rectangular blocks have set the basic city design.

In the 1790s, L'Enfant's plans were exhibited in Paris, where they would have been seen as innovative and on an impressive scale. There is no evidence that L'Enfant's design for Washington had a direct influence on events in his home country, but large-scale city-design issues were a very relevant concern in France at the time. After the execution of Louis XVI in 1793, the Revolutionary Commune confiscated all royal land and appointed a Commission of Artists to replan Paris. The commission made the first detailed proposals for creating grand avenues and cutting long, straight streets through the densely inhabited parts of the city.

When Napoleon took power in 1799, he began implementing these proposals, notably the Rue de Rivoli, designed by Charles Percier and Pierre Fontaine in 1801, which created the street frontage facing the Tuileries Gardens. The ground floor of the buildings facing the street was given over to an arcade and shops. The houses above had two principal floors, then a top story and an attic. The elevation was designed to be a series of simple, repeating elements with no center or end pavilions.

Despite the hints available from painting, stage scenery and individual buildings, it had never been clear just how the long, straight avenues that Fontana, Wren and L'Enfant drew would be designed in three dimensions. Here was one fully realized avenue frontage of uniform architecture, but it was not necessarily what would have been designed at an earlier period.

The modular, repetitive design of the Rue de Rivoli buildings was in many respects the outcome of the turmoil in French architectural theory and education during the 1790s. As part of the changes brought on by the revolution, the old architectural academy was suppressed, although its school continued to function at a reduced level and Charles Percier was one of the teachers. However, a new school was created, L'École Polytechnique, whose professor of architecture from 1795 to 1830 was Jean-Nicolas-Louis Durand.

The Polytechnique was primarily an engineering school, born partly of the need the revolutionary government, surrounded by hostile monarchies, felt for a great many military engineers in a hurry.

J.-N.-L. Durand's course at the Polytechnique and his textbook, *Précis de Leçons d'Architecture,* first published between 1802 and 1805, undertook to simplify and codify the nature of architecture.

Instead of architecture as Leone Battista Alberti had written about it at the end of the fifteenth century, where the building's organization and proportion became a subtle system embodying what were believed to be the underlying harmonies of the universe, Durand classified the design of buildings according to type and created a system of arrangement for the parts of a building that was based on a simple, modular grid.

Perhaps Durand was motivated by the need to jam as much architecture as possible into the heads of his engineering students, but—at least in its early years—the Polytechnique was seen as providing a revolutionary alternative to the architectural design pursued by the ancien régime.

Whatever its motivation, Durand's course, with its clearly articulated rules and easily repeated patterns, was well suited to the temperament of the late eighteenth and early nineteenth centuries, an important period in the development of modern science and engineering, and a time when changes in cities were happening at a rapid pace and on an unprecedented scale.

These first effects of industrialization on cities, at the beginning of the nineteenth century, were very largely positive, the result of the tremendous increase in wealth, reflected in large numbers of new houses for the middle and upper classes. The pollution, overcrowding and other negative effects of industry were to come to the cities later, after the development of railway networks in the 1830s. The first factories were located near sources of water power. As the cities of the time were almost always built near navigable waterways, and the presence of waterfalls is not helpful to navigation, industry almost always began well away from existing cities.

Cities began to grow, following the pattern already visible at Covent Garden in the 1630s: estates on the fashionable side of the city were subdivided, and the houses sold to rich people whose social standing was one notch below that of the estate owners and who wished to enjoy the prestige of the address. Later, commerce followed the carriage trade; and shops, also looking for prestige, invaded fashionable residential districts. Often, as at Covent Garden, the rich moved on, and the whole district became commercial.

In Great Britain and North America this pattern emerged earlier than in Europe, where urban growth was inhibited by fortifications. The expansion of fashionable areas in American cities usually took the form of a street of mansions leading out of the city center up a hill or toward some other desirable location: Beacon Hill in Boston, Hillhouse Avenue in New Haven, Broadway in New York City, Charles Street in Baltimore.

England, where the new industrial development was strongest, enjoyed the most marked increase in wealth, and the whole West End of London grew rapidly as a series of streets and squares of stylish houses. John Nash was the architect who did the most to give this new expansion a designed form, and he managed to synthesize the incremental growth that characterized London real-estate development with the long vistas which had long been part of the theory of city design but had not previously been achieved in London.

Nash became an official royal architect in 1806 and his most important opportunity followed in 1811, when the prince regent (whose father, George III, was still alive but certified as a lunatic and kept discreetly out of the way) asked Nash to prepare a plan for a large tract of undeveloped Crown land which was then on the edge of London's rapid westward expansion.

Nash had a difficult problem because the royal lands were north of the existing fashionable district and could not be developed successfully without a new street that would connect them southward to the important parts of London. The only practical route was through the edge of a poor neighborhood adjoining fashionable areas that had already been built up to the west. The irregular route did not permit the long, straight street that in theory had become the standard vocabulary of city design, and the amount of land involved was far too large to be undertaken by a single developer.

Nash's design for Regent Street is a brilliant work of invention and coordination. Lower Regent Street begins at what was originally the site of Carlton House, the prince regent's residence, and a new square just to the north, Waterloo Place. From Waterloo Place the street runs north to a series of intersections at Piccadilly Circus, this circus an application of the Woods' innovation at Bath. Regent Street then switches westward in a reverse curve, the Quadrant, runs not quite straight northward and crosses Oxford Street at another circus. Just to the north, the succession of streets turns westward again, where the transition is marked by the spire of All Souls, Langham Place, and meets Great Portland Street, which leads north to a crescent that is the gateway to the new quarter that Nash designed, Regent's Park.

Regent's Park is another impressive design formulation. Nash planned this district in a way that anticipated the development of garden-city design principles, which we will consider in the next chapter. Instead of a repeating pattern of street and square, Nash created a large park, like the grounds of a country estate, which was to serve as a greenbelt between the rows of houses around the outer edge and a circular cluster of development near the center. Around the northern perimeter of the park there was a canal, which served a market district in the southeast portion of the Regent's property.

The development of Regent's Park was never fully achieved, but Nash was able to oversee the completion of the whole length of Regent Street. This success helped prompt the regent, now King George IV, to move to Buckingham Palace and tear down Carlton House, opening a prime development frontage on St. James's Park, which was then also designed by Nash.

Nash as an architect has been accused of unrolling his facades like wallpaper to cover his large-scale architectural compositions, and because most of the work was executed in stucco, it has often been considered inferior to buildings constructed of stone. It is true that many of the buildings along Regent Street could be accused of lacking studied refinement of detail, but in many cases Nash, as the entrepreneur who was putting the development of the whole street together, achieved the coordination of these buildings through diplomacy and did not design them directly himself. Nash managed to keep the control of the critical facades that close vistas or are important accents when the street system changes direction, and he seldom overlooked any architectural element that was needed to ensure the continuity of the whole composition.

There was also a change of sensibility involved, which parallels the changes in architecture being advocated by J.-N.-L. Durand at the same time. The use of regular, repeating elements may have been partly the result of large-scale and rapid execution, but it is also an intellectual and aesthetic choice.

As a piece of three-dimensional city design, Regent Street was unprecedented in its day, and has seldom been equaled. Trystan Edwards was one of the earliest commentators to appreciate Nash's contribution to London. In an essay written in 1923, while most of Nash's Regent Street was being demolished to make way for larger buildings, Edwards sought to answer Nash's critics with a defense of stucco as an admirably unifying building material which also reflects light beautifully; and followed his defense of stucco by an analysis of the devices, such as the spacing between windows and the ratios of window to wall, that Nash used to maintain unity among his facades. Today, Nash's abilities are understood and appreciated; and most of his London buildings that have survived redevelopment and war damage have been restored; but Nash's Regent Street is gone. The street layout remains, but the new architecture lacks the original unity that came from the careful relationships of part to part and building to street.

Louis Napoleon, exiled to London, admired Regent Street and Nash's long rows of palatial house facades fronting on parks and gardens; when he returned to Paris and took power as Emperor Napoleon III, he hoped to be able to create equivalents there.

The long, straight streets of the 1793 commission plan were said to have appealed to the first Napoleon as a means of keeping down the unruly Paris mob, and the same motive has been attributed to Napoleon III, who handed a map of priority street improvements to Georges-Eugène Haussmann, the energetic administrator he had just appointed prefect of the Seine.

Haussmann did cite riot control as one of the advantages of the proposed new street system in a presentation to the Paris city council soon after he took office, but other major aims were slum clearance and traffic improvement, particularly connecting the newly constructed railway stations to each other and to the important central destinations. Whatever military advantages the new street system possessed did not prevent the rising of the Paris Commune in 1871.

Haussmann had seventeen years to carry out the transformation of Paris, including not only new streets and buildings but a comprehensive reconstruction of the water supply, a new sewer system and extensive park improvements.

It was Haussmann who took the concept of the long, straight urban street—whose history by this time went back more than three centuries —and applied it for the first time in a systematic way to the redesign of an existing city. He made use of what we would today call excess condemnation, taking enough land not only for the right-of-way of the new street but for property development on either side. This property was sold to developers with restrictions that ensured a uniform series of facades.

The basic building type for these new streets had shops on the ground floor, following the precedent of the Napoleonic Rue de Rivoli, and shops and offices on a mezzanine, if there was one. Instead of dividing the frontage vertically into individual houses, as was done in London or in Parisian squares like the Place des Vosges and the Place Vendôme, Haussmann used a large block divided horizontally. There would be three floors of spacious apartments, with smaller dwellings at the attic level, and even smaller rooms in a second attic, seven flights up. The facades were designed to express these horizontal divisions, with belt courses, balconies and cornices, while rows of regularly spaced french windows imparted their rhythm to the street.

The new streets were broad boulevards with ample sidewalks that left room for rows of trees—an aspect of Haussmann's formulation learned, perhaps, from Versailles, but more probably from Nash and the gardens maintained in English squares since the end of the eighteenth century. An urban street lined with trees was a concept that would have been foreign to Sixtus V or Christopher Wren. Sometimes there was a garden with trees in the center of the Parisian boulevard as well. Haussmann would often arrange for full-grown trees to be transplanted to the new boulevards, giving a sense of completeness to raw, new districts. The parks designed by Haussmann's landscape engineer, Jean Alphand, were important parts of the overall plan for Paris. Alphand took the kidney-shaped paths and artfully informal vistas of English gardening and applied them in a systematic way that was more French than English. The Bois de Boulogne and the Bois de Vincennes were to have been joined by a greenbelt that would have surrounded the whole city after the walls were taken down, but Haussmann was unable to muster the political support for this aspect of his plan.

Haussmann's methods were high-handed, but he did operate in an environment of law. The courts set the compensation that had to be paid to owners of properties that were expropriated, and that compensation was at least fair, and has been criticized for being too generous, allowing unreasonable profits to real-estate speculators.

The money for property acquisition and construction was borrowed against future revenues that would result from the increased property values created by the planned improvements, a principle similar to modern theories about value recapture and tax-increment financing. As time went on, however, Haussmann began to borrow the money first and leave the legalities to be worked out later, and his attempts to evade legislative oversight led him to borrow on a dangerously short time scale.

Haussmann's plans were so comprehensive that he eventually made too many political enemies, particularly when his new streets began to invade the fashionable western district of Paris. As Napoleon III's political control began to weaken, Haussmann's record of mounting debts and unauthorized public expenditures put him in a more and more exposed position, until he was forced out of office in 1870. Haussmann thought he was working for an emperor. He failed to understand the transition to democratic institutions that was taking place behind the facade of absolutist rule.

Haussmann has been criticized as a vandal who destroyed the historic urban texture of Paris, but the Paris beloved by tourists is very much Haussmann's city. Haussmann has also been praised for making one last heroic effort to impart a rational order to the process of nineteenth-century urbanization, which was rapidly moving out of control; but in the end his effort was only partially successful.

Haussmann's redesign of Paris was a summation of the monumental city-design principles that had been evolving since the Renaissance. It was their first comprehensive application to a major existing city; it was also in a very real sense the last. Despite the enormous influence of Haussmann's boulevards on cities throughout the world, monumental design principles rapidly passed from being a practical city-design technique to a utopian concept.

It was not their association with dictatorial power that made monumental city-design ideas so difficult to implement. Robert Moses, the manager of New York City's slum clearance and its park and highway construction for more than four decades, who evidently considered himself a successor to Haussmann and a kindred spirit, reviewed Haussmann's career in an article published in 1942. Moses's conclusion was that Haussmann's methods were perfectly applicable in a modern democratic society, and that Haussmann's personal debacle could have been avoided if he had paid more attention to public opinion and legislative fence mending. Robert Moses's own operating procedures look unacceptably high-handed from today's perspective, but it is true that major changes continue to be carried out in modern cities. There also, unfortunately, continues to be no shortage of dictators, but Haussmann's Paris came to seem a more and more unobtainable vision.

The events that undermined monumental city design were the invention of the passenger elevator, followed by the decentralization of cities brought on by the automobile.

Monumental city design is based on the unspoken assumption that no building will be taller than the maximum distance people will walk up stairs, and that districts will be developed gradually at a relatively uniform density. The elevator permitted a direct expression of underlying land values; building owners could choose almost any height they wanted. The railroad began the process of urban decentralization, although development continued to center on the railway stations. The automobile permitted development to skip from one location to another, based on such relatively random factors as the availability of property and the permissiveness of authorities.

It is possible to maintain building heights and densities by means of codes, as was done in Paris, but codes become harder to enforce the more they run contrary to economic realities.

The most direct illustration of the conflict between monumental city design and modern technology and economics is the history of the City Beautiful movement in the United States.

The coalescence of Beaux Arts architecture and Haussmannesque planning principles into the City Beautiful movement began with the great public success of the design for the central group of buildings at the World's Columbian Exposition, held in Chicago in 1893. The architects for the buildings in the Court of Honor around the central lagoon agreed to follow an arrangement designed by the landscape architect Frederick L. Olmsted and his young associate, Henry Codman; to employ a similar architectural vocabulary, based on French academic classicism; and to coordinate such elements as axes of symmetry and cornice lines. During the design process two of the architectural firms also voluntarily omitted central domed elements from their buildings because they competed with the dominance of Richard Morris Hunt's administration building at the head of the lagoon.

This exhibition, with its enormous architectural and civic spaces quickly built in lath and plaster, was intended by its designers to demonstrate both what city design could and should be like and to show the American public what an appropriate civic character for their cities might be. A traditional role for architects has been to assist arriviste clients in creating a background and setting appropriate to their newly achieved status. The United States was a newly rich nation, and the architects of the 1893 fair wished to help it achieve an instant cultural heritage.

The fair made Daniel Burnham, its coordinating architect, into a national figure. He was elected president of the American Institute of Architects, which led to an involvement in the politics of governmental architecture, and eventually to the chairmanship of the Senate Park Commission, set up in 1901 at the initiative of Senator James McMillan, chairman of the Senate's District of Columbia Committee.

The other members of the commission were Frederick Law Olmsted, Jr., who had taken over the direction of the family firm when his father retired in 1895, and Charles F. McKim of McKim, Mead and White, who had probably the most subtle architectural intelligence involved in the design of the Chicago fair and who had become a strong friend of Burnham's.

The Park Commission's plan, usually called the McMillan plan, restored and elaborated upon L'Enfant's original design, and became the basis for planning most of the monumental government buildings in Washington during the next forty years, notably the Federal Triangle and the Lincoln and Jefferson memorials. Burnham succeeded in negotiating the railway tracks and station out of the Mall in front of the Capitol, the railroads agreeing to create Union Station north of Capitol Hill as a replacement, and the government agreeing to finance a tunnel to take the tracks under the Mall. The Mall itself was replanned in harmony with the French garden design that must have been L'Enfant's intention, removing various accretions, including Andrew Jackson Downing's picturesque English garden in front of the Smithsonian, and bending the Mall slightly, to place the Washington Monument—which, because of foundation problems, was built off both the Capitol and the White House axes—in the center of the Mall. McKim drew elaborate plans, which have never been implemented, to create a setting for the Washington Monument that would also recognize the axis from the White House. As noted earlier, McKim's design for the placement of the Lincoln Memorial and the Tidal Basin closed the vistas from the White House and the Capitol that L'Enfant had daringly left open, making the overall composition of monumental Washington much more self-contained and static, in the same way that McKim closed the axis of Jefferson's University of Virginia with a group of three additional buildings.

However, the most important action to ensure the preservation of the L'Enfant plan and the design continuity of monumental Washington was taken in 1899, by Senator McMillan's District of Columbia Committee, when Congress enacted height limits of 60 feet for non-fireproof construction, 90 feet for any building on a residential street, and 130 feet for buildings on the widest streets. It is not at all clear that Burnham understood the critical importance of this enactment in preserving the validity of a monumental city-design concept for Washington. The height-limit issue would have been settled by the time the commission began work, and there was probably little demand for tall buildings in Washington at the time or up to the Second World War. Since then there have been many proposals to break the Washington height limit, but so far, the limit has been retained, with only minor modifications.

The height issue was critical to the success or failure of Burnham's Chicago plan, which was published in 1909. It was the most famous plan of the City Beautiful movement and a pivotal document in the history of city design.

By the time Burnham was asked to prepare a plan for his home city, he had designed a civic center for Cleveland, plans for Manila and its summer capital at Baguio, and, with Edward Bennett, a plan for San Francisco that was completed and accepted just the day before the great earthquake and fire of 1906. The San Francisco plan was a comprehensive design in which a group of civic buildings on Market Street became the focal point for Haussmannesque avenues radiating to all points in the city. The earthquake and fire made it more difficult to implement a comprehensive plan. As in London in 1666, the top priority was to get the city in operation again, not to reorganize it. However, the civic center group was later constructed much as proposed in the plan, although in a slightly different location, and some elements of the park plan were also carried out.

Although the purpose of Burnham and Bennett's Chicago plan was civic beautification, the underlying traffic and transportation issues were carefully studied. The plan placed an overlay of Parisian boulevards on Chicago's existing gridiron street system and, by reorganizing the railroad lines, cleared the lakefront for a series of monumental parks. Chicago owes its beautiful lakefront and the boulevard character of Michigan Avenue to this plan, which was well promoted through an extensive public relations campaign. However, there was no mechanism like the Washington height limit that would supplement the persuasive power of the plan itself and require private investors to follow its directions. The legal opinion that forms the final chapter of the Chicago plan, written by Walter L. Fisher, saw no legal obstacles to the construction of the parks, public buildings and new streets, other than a need for legislation that would greatly increase the city's powers to borrow money. Walter Fisher was doubtful, though, about the applicability of the excess condemnation system that Haussmann had used in Paris, wondering whether such land takings could be justified as a public purpose. The opinion concludes that the problem could be solved if enabling legislation would be passed by the State of Illinois, although there seems to be some equivocation about whether the federal courts would find the state action constitutional. Zoning ordinances had already been enacted in Europe, and studies toward the New York City zoning ordinance were to begin only four years later, but neither Fisher nor anyone else seems to have thought of zoning as an implementation mechanism for monumental plans.

Burnham had to know that the tall building posed a problem to his monumental designs. His own office was continuously producing tall buildings during all the years that he worked on his city plans. The Chicago plan attempts to deal with this issue by setting uniform heights for elevator buildings, but there is no enforcement mechanism, and uniform height regulations run counter to the great variations in real estate values to be found in Chicago's business districts.

None of the numerous plans for cities produced under the influence of the City Beautiful movement between the 1893 fair and the 1932 economic depression found a successful means to incorporate the tall building and other types of private investment into the design. As a result, these plans have left as legacies park systems and groups of monumental government buildings, but only Washington was given a single, coherent image, because of the height limit and because the monumental center sets so much of its character.

Walter Burley Griffin and Marion Mahony Griffin, architects and landscape architects from Chicago (and former employees of Frank Lloyd Wright), won an international competition for the design of Canberra, the new capital of Australia, in 1912. (Eliel Saarinen's design was placed second, and that of Frenchman D. Alf. Agache third.) Their design was essentially a garden city, and we will come back to it in the next chapter, but there was a monumental center to the plan, which is as powerful in its way as the design structure of Burnham and Bennett's Chicago plan. Like L'Enfant, the Griffins used topography as the basis for geometric organization. Three hills, denoted the capitol, the civic center and the market center, are connected by long, straight streets to form an equilateral triangle. The capitol is treated as the vertex, and a straight line, the land axis, runs from the capitol, bisecting the triangle, crosses the municipal axis, which is the base of the triangle, and extends to Mount Ainslie, a prominent landscape feature at the boundary of the city. Halfway between the vertex and the base of the triangle is the water axis, running through a basin, which was intended to be symmetrically disposed about the land axis. The water fills the valley between the three hills and then continues in both directions along the dammed-up Molonglo River valley. The part of the triangle nearest the vertex was the site for the government buildings, grouped symmetrically around the land axis.

New Delhi, the planned British capital of India, is also a garden city with a monumental center. The Griffins' design plus seven more premiated entries in the Canberra competition were available to Edwin Lutyens, Herbert Baker and the other members of the Delhi Town Planning Committee during the formative stages of their work, which was completed at the end of March 1913. This original Delhi plan, which was later modified to permit the addition of a parliament house not at first contemplated in the imperial program, has some strong resemblances to the geometric organization of the Griffins' design, although there are many important differences.

The main axis of New Delhi lies approximately east-west, centering on the viceroy's palace and the administrative secretariat, which are placed atop the highest land mass in the immediate area. A line drawn north-south through the secretariat buildings forms the base of two equilateral triangles. The western triangle encloses the viceroy's palace and gardens; at the vertex of the eastern triangle is a memorial arch that lies at the end of a monumental avenue that runs up the hill, passes between the secretariat buildings and terminates at the viceroy's palace. A cross-axis halfway down the main avenue runs northward to a circular commercial center, Connaught Place—which is in many ways analogous to Canberra's civic center—and forms the vertex of a larger equilateral triangle which encloses the entire monumental government complex. There is another important line of sight at sixty degrees to the main avenue, which connects the secretariats through Connaught Place to the Jama Masjid, the great mosque in the center of old Delhi. When the parliament building was added, it was placed on this Jama Masjid axis, just to the northeast of the secretariat buildings.

The palace and secretariat at New Delhi are now recognized as one of the great architectural achievements of the twentieth century. Lutyens and Baker were able to attain a vitality in their monumental architecture that has eluded most other modern practitioners, perhaps because their program was a thoroughly traditional one, for an autocracy that was already an anachronism when construction began.

The main avenue between the secretariats was the cause of a well-known dispute between Lutyens, the architect of the viceroy's palace and master designer of the whole city, and his associate, Baker, the architect of the secretariats. Lutyens had misunderstood a section drawing, and approved it without realizing that the great processional east-west road would lose its view of the viceroy's palace as it ran between the secretariats, because of the steepness of the grade. By the time Lutyens made his initial protest, it was decided that too many commitments had been made, and the slope could not be corrected. Lutyens persisted in trying to reverse this decision for years, pulling every string at his command, but without success. Although the decision not to change the gradient was made for financial reasons, it was also an aesthetic issue. Baker, who had made the design for the steeply sloping avenue, never saw anything wrong with it.

Lutyen's principal reason for objecting to the gradient of the main avenue was that by obscuring the viceroy's palace it destroyed the sense of spatial enclosure that should be created by the ensemble of palace and secretariats, as well as diminishing the symbolic importance of the vice-roy, whose palace should be continuously perceived as the apex of the composition.

The Lutyens-Baker dispute recalls Camillo Sitte's critique of Haussmannesque planning, *City Building According to Artistic Principles,* first published in Vienna in 1889.

Sitte was the head of government schools for artisans in Salzburg and then Vienna, and a champion of the craft tradition. He sought by analysis of the great civic spaces of the past to deduce the principles on which they were designed. While his book includes many medieval town squares, Sitte was equally interested in the great Renaissance plazas. For Sitte, the emphasis placed on the long avenue, which had dominated city design since Sixtus V and would seem to be the essence of most City Beautiful plans, was nowhere near as important as the enclosure of spaces at appropriate scales. The point of conflict occurs at spaces that terminate avenues. Sitte believed that the appropriate enclosure of the space took precedence over the views of important buildings seen down radiating avenues. He particularly objected to the siting of a building like the Paris Opera, which is an island in the middle of intersecting streets. Sitte argued that important buildings of this kind deserved their own enclosed precinct, and his book contains diagrams of the way in which the Votivkirche and other significant buildings in Vienna could be improved by being given what he believed would be an appropriate context of smaller surrounding structures.

Because Sitte's book helped bring about a revival of interest in medieval city forms, he is sometimes classified as a romantic and a champion of winding streets and irregular spaces. In his own work as a planning practitioner, however, Sitte showed himself to be interested both in orderly traffic flow and in minimizing practical problems like land assembly. He was perfectly capable of using straight streets and rectangular city blocks where they suited his purpose. Sitte's greatest influence, nevertheless, was over the picturesque architectural compositions created for garden cities and garden suburbs.

Sitte had no more to say about the tall building than Haussmann; but for many years the existence of the elevator did not seem to pose an immediate city-planning issue in most countries. During the period between the two world wars, tall buildings were a relative rarity except in North America, and even the modern architecture built in the center of older cities was usually of a type that would fit into the prevailing street frontage with very little disturbance of established patterns.

In the United States, however, the tall building continued to disrupt received concepts of city design. The first of them, like Louis Sullivan's Prudential and Wainwright buildings, had been constructed with architectural ornament only on the street frontages. Somehow it was expected that eventually all buildings would be at the new height, so that there was no point wasting money on the sides and back. By the 1920s it was well understood that tall buildings required greater spacing than row houses or Parisian apartment blocks, and that traditional monumental arrangements had to be modified to accommodate the new heights.

New York City's first zoning ordinance, adopted in 1916, made a simplified version of monumental planning into a legal necessity. Buildings were required to be set back from the building line when they attained a height that was mathematically related to the width of the street. The near-uniformity of the lower portions of apartment buildings facing Central Park, Riverside Park or Park Avenue that were built under the 1916 ordinance (it was revised completely in 1961) created something akin to the Parisian boulevard, although nowhere near as uniform and on a much larger scale.

In Manhattan's midtown and Wall Street districts, zoning was less successful in creating design continuity. The framers of the ordinance had recognized that the logical result of setback requirements was that all buildings would have to taper to floor sizes that made less and less economic sense. Using Cass Gilbert's 1913 Woolworth Building as a model, the zoning was written so that once a tower had set back to a point where it filled 25 percent of the lot area or less, it could continue straight up without further modification.

The mass and height of towers was thus related to the size of property that developers could put together, rather than to a relationship with a continuous element like a street. Because of the large size of the property on which it is built, Rockefeller Center, designed in its current form in 1931, is one of the few significant attempts within the New York City zoning ordinance to organize a group of tall buildings of various heights. The design, led by Raymond Hood of the associated offices of Reinhard & Hofmeister; Corbett, Harrison and MacMurray; and Hood and Fouilhoux placed two pairs of six-story buildings on Fifth Avenue to frame the axis of the RCA and Associated Press buildings. The concept of a tall tower related by an axis to a forecourt is close to the monumental tradition, even when the tower is seventy stories high, but there is no comparable logic in the relationship between the dominant RCA building and the other tall structures in the complex.

In the 1930s the worldwide economic depression shifted the focus of city design from private investment to the activities of governments. Monumental architectural groups continued to be the preferred expression for governmental buildings, although, as we will see in Chapter 4, this was the period of experimentation with modernist ideas of city design in subsidized housing and other government projects.

However, Nazi ideology considered modern architecture decadent, and also questioned the tall building and even steel-frame construction. Adolf Hitler, who had been turned down for admission to the School of Architecture at Vienna's Academy of Fine Arts, frequently stopped in at the studio of Albert Speer, his official architect, to check on the progress of the 1939 plan for Berlin and to make suggestions of his own. Hitler greatly admired Haussmann's Paris and the monumental buildings of Vienna's Ringstrasse, and he sought to surpass them in his own capital.

The Berlin plan was in many respects like other city plans of the period. Its monumental sequence of boulevards lined with governmental and corporate administration buildings was to be achieved without otherwise changing the fabric of the city. Land was assembled by the government, and then individual parcels were assigned to different official agencies or sold to private industries interested in a showcase location for their corporate headquarters. There was a functional purpose to the boulevard design, as it was linked to a plan for rationalizing the railroad system, and there was a major railroad terminal at each end of the new boulevard sequence.

Speer's New State Chancellery of 1937 was not radically different from the architecture of other capital cities in the 1930s, including Washington, D.C.; and much of the government architecture planned for the new boulevards was similarly conventional, as were private buildings, such as Peter Behrens's projected headquarters building for AEG. Only the enormous scale of the whole project, and the great hall and triumphal arch, betray underlying megalomania. Speer asserted that the arch and great hall were to be paid for by private donations, a sinister statement in view of the expropriation of the property of Jews that was going on at the time the plan was being drawn, along with the grand plans for foreign conquests.

The identification of monumental architecture with Nazi and fascist ideology and with authoritarianism in general helps explain the widespread revulsion against monumental city planning ideas after the Second World War, although the major reasons for the change were the emergence of the tall building as a major ingredient in almost all cities, and the increasing influence of the automobile in dispersing the uniform densities that once prevailed in city centers. However, the modern architecture that replaced monumental design almost everywhere had never evolved large-scale design concepts to take the place of the boulevard, the square or the axis of symmetry; and no system of modulating facades ever completely replaced the column and the arch. As a result, architects faced with the problem of creating a group of buildings continued to use academic principles of composition, although in many cases—such as Lincoln Center in New York City—the impression given is that the monumental composition was a fallback position, used for lack of any better idea.

There has since been a strong revival of interest in monumental city design, often as a way of constructing a critique of modern architecture. Part of this interest in monumental principles of city design is traceable to Colin Rowe, professor at Cornell University, who has taught an entire generation of architects not to ignore the importance of the street, the axis and the role of building mass as the definer of urban space. Rowe has also been an articulate critic of the strong utopian component in modernism, which caused many of its adherents to believe that older cities could and should be swept away. Rowe and Fred Koetter published a critique of modernist city design, entitled *Collage City,* first in the August 1975 *Architectural Review* and then, in a somewhat more complex version, as a book in 1978.

Rowe and Koetter's basic point is that city design is a great deal more like collage than like drawing on a clean sheet of paper, and the city designer should use the materials at hand, including the existing development of the city to date, and transform them into a new design. There was, however, a strong bias in favor of examples of monumental city design in the illustrations chosen.

The figure-ground map is one of Colin Rowe's favorite didactic techniques. Giambattista Nolli's 1748 map of Rome has often been used by Rowe as a prototype. Nolli showed all buildings in plan as solid masses except for courtyards and major interior spaces. The texture of the map makes space read as a positive quality, the obverse of the building mass. Of course, this effect comes not just from the map technique but from the nature of Rome in the mid-eighteenth century, with its closely spaced buildings of essentially uniform height.

In 1978 Michael Graves, then architect-in-residence at the American Academy in Rome, invited twelve architects, including Colin Rowe, to take one of the twelve segments of the Nolli map and redesign that segment of Rome in any way they chose. Indicating that what was implied was the kind of interpolation or collage technique advocated by Rowe, the event was called "Roma Interrotta," which might be interpreted as "Interventions in Rome after a lapse of time." The results, not surprisingly, were extremely diverse. James Stirling used variants of his own buildings to compose his sector. Rowe and his associates made a drawing that might have been the Nolli map itself, except for the regularity and repetitive quality of the new elements. Perhaps the most unexpected interpolations were those designed by Leon Krier, who modified St. Peter's Square, the Via Corso, the Campidoglio and the Piazza Navona with different versions of the same structure: a long-span hipped roof supported on columns that were actually individual buildings, each about seven or eight stories high but with a floor plan only large enough for one artist's studio per floor.

Leon Krier's drawings for Roma Interrotta seem to mark a transition in his work from the design of projects for monumental, symmetrical megastructures ("megastructures" in the sense in which they will be discussed in Chapter 5) to monumental city design of a somewhat more conventional kind. Krier's projects are both more and less antiquarian than his early-nineteenth-century presentation style would lead one to expect. He favors plans in which monumental boulevards section off districts into strongly articulated precincts, more regular than in a medieval city but just as distinct. In this way his plans resemble the texture of Paris, where Haussmann's boulevards cut through the preexisting fabric of the city, and do not resemble Washington, or Burnham's plan for Chicago, where the boulevards are an overlay on a continuous, regular grid pattern.

Leon Krier also seems to accept Camillo Sitte's critique of Haussmann, and by extension of earlier Baroque plans, in considering the enclosure of space more important than the vista. He often makes the intersection of two major boulevards take place in a monumental, covered outdoor space where the roof is supported by a group of buildings, a totally nontraditional concept that was not even technically possible until the late nineteenth century.

Rob Krier, Leon Krier's older brother, a professor at the Technical University in Vienna, has published a series of projects for monumental city designs that appear to carry on the development of the city as if the tall building and the modernist revolution in architecture had never happened. More traditional than Leon Krier, he shows a rich variety of urban spaces and gardens, and is also adept at fitting the small rooms of a modern apartment within a palatial building form.

Another city designer who has come to monumental design via an investigation of megastructures is the Barcelona architect Ricardo Bofill. His point of departure might well be Adolph Loos's entry in the Chicago Tribune competition of 1922, a tall office building in the form of a gigantic Doric column. This project has long been an embarrassment to historians of modern architecture, who counted Loos as a pioneer of a new sensibility. They hoped that the column was really a joke, but it was all too evident that Loos was perfectly serious.

Bofill has taken this architectural dead end and turned it into a medium of expression, creating whole building groups whose component parts are columns and entablatures at an enormously inflated scale. At least in theory, this is one way in which monumental city-design principles could be employed to organize tall buildings, but the result is really a megastructure; and Bofill himself seems to be moving away from monumental giantism to a more traditional kind of monumental organization.

In the end, however, consideration of recent monumental projects has to come down to the way they treat the tall building, and the essence of most such work is that the kind of tall building made possible by the steel frame, or reinforced concrete, has only a very limited place in city design. It can be used sparingly, as an accent, but the urban texture has to be that of the city before the invention of the elevator and the Bessemer process for mass-producing steel.

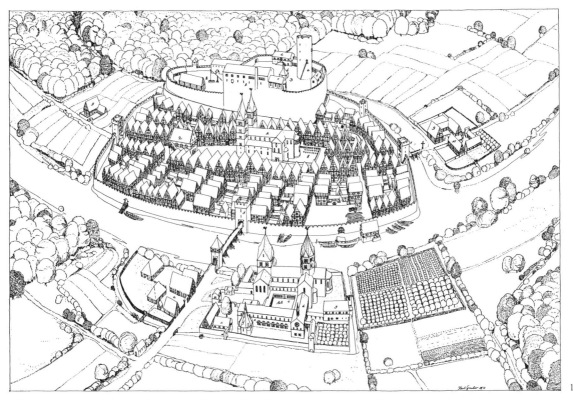

1, 2: Karl Gruber's drawings of the evolution of a hypothetical German city, first as it was in 1180, then in 1350, from his book *Ein Deutscher Stadt.*

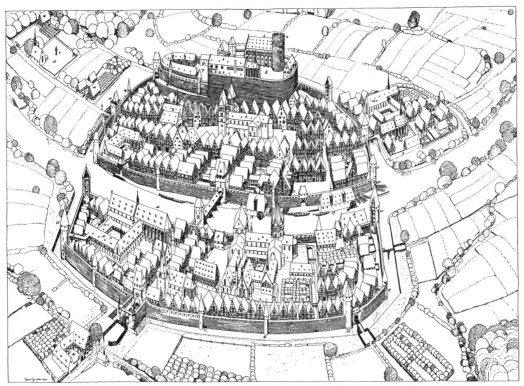

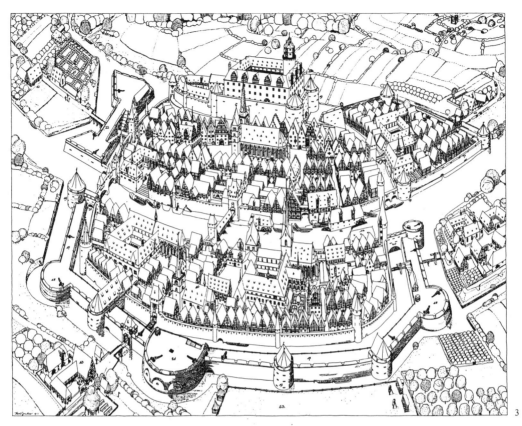

3: The third drawing in Gruber's sequence, the same city in 1580. These drawings illustrate the relatively slow development of cities before the Renaissance; the city grows, the fortifications are improved, cathedral and castle are rebuilt, but it is recognizably the same city four centuries later.

4: Hogenberg's map of London, published in 1572, shows a typical medieval city comparable to Gruber's. The major difference is that England's island location and Elizabethan sea power had permitted London's development to extend beyond the fortifications.

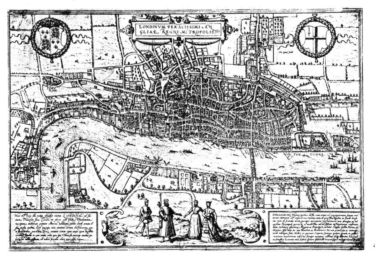

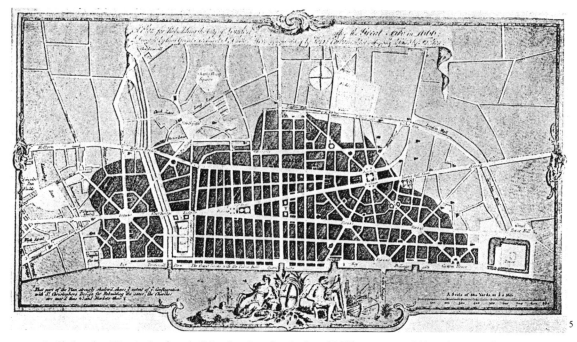

5: Christopher Wren's plan for rebuilding London after the fire of 1666 was more ambitious than any other urban plan up to that time. It would have created a complete Renaissance city but involved too complex an exchange of property to be carried out. Wren, a scholar and scientist before he became an architect, derived his ideas from books and maps describing the already well-established design formulations in Italy and France. The ideas used in this plan were as different from the organization of the medieval city as Wren's architecture was from late Gothic building traditions.

6

6: Elbert Peets's evocation of what Wren's London might have looked like entered from the west, with the new St. Paul's directly in view, framed by the two main, radiating avenues.

7

7, 8: The design of Michelangelo's building group, the Capitol, in Rome. The two flanking buildings are canted, as in a stage set, to create an exaggerated perspective vista. Michelangelo also strengthened the perspective effect by giving the two buildings a uniform architecture, based on his inventive use of pilasters extending from the base of the building to the cornice. The plan and perspective are from Paul Letarouilly's *Edifices de Rome Moderne.*

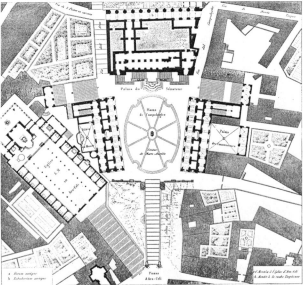

8

9: An example of actual Baroque stage scenery: a street in Siena, by Bartolomeo Neroni, 1560. Renaissance concepts of urban space, derived from an understanding of perspective, appeared first in paintings, then in scene designs.

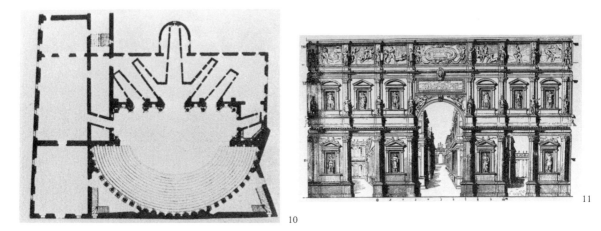

10, 11: The Teatro Olimpico in Vicenza, designed by Andrea Palladio, has a permanent stage set by Palladio's pupil Vincenzo Scamozzi, which shows, through a central arch and four side doors, glimpses of seven streets lined with buildings of a uniform architecture vanishing in an exaggerated perspective.

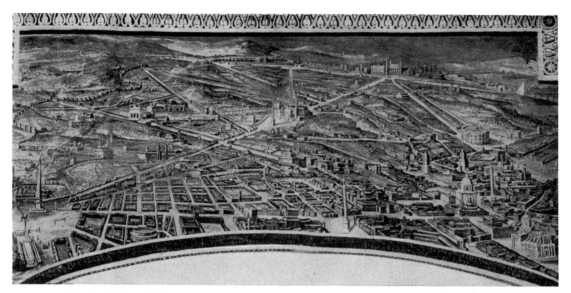

12, 13: This fresco in the Vatican Library made during the reign of Pope Sixtus V shows his plans for Rome, in which long avenues with vistas terminated by obelisks link the principal pilgrimage points in the city. The design for the Piazza del Popolo, lower left in the fresco and shown in detail below, not fully realized until the nineteenth century, shows streets that converge on a central point, from which a visitor to the city is given a series of perspective views like those in the Baroque theater. In his London plan, Wren used a similar device at the end of London Bridge, and his proposal to place a rebuilt St. Paul's at the origin of two major avenues would seem to show that Wren was familiar with the way Carlo Rainaldi's twin churches, begun in 1662, frame the streets fanning out from the Piazza del Popolo.

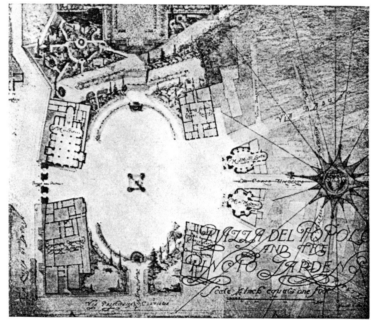

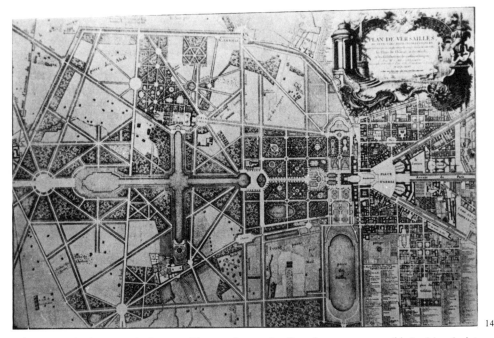

14: Baroque landscape gardening was able to realize scenic effects that were not possible in cities. André le Nôtre was at work on the plans for Versailles when Christopher Wren visited France in 1665. Wren's London plan indicates that he probably saw these drawings, as well as le Nôtre's earlier work at Vaux le Vicomte. Le Nôtre used a fan of three streets on the town side of Versailles, but gave the central position to the monarch rather than to the arriving visitor. The park at Versailles is organized along a major axis that extends out over the landscape; from this axis subsidiary vistas cut through the forest. Some of these pathways meet other forest paths in circular intersections, ronds-points, which have their origin in the rituals of the royal hunt. Wren was to apply these circular intersections to city design in his London plan.

15: This mid-eighteenth-century scene design, *The Elysian Fields,* by Fabrizio Galliari, illustrates the kind of landscape found in a Baroque hunting forest, scenic vistas fanning out from a central viewing point.

16: This sketch by Elbert Peets of the city square at Leghorn (Livorno) in Italy shows a completely realized Renaissance square that was known to Inigo Jones, the architect for the first such square in England, Covent Garden, 17. The residential square became the bourgeois counterpoise to the assertion of royal power made by axis and vista. A group of relatively small individual houses combined have an architectural presence equivalent to the courtyard of a palace.

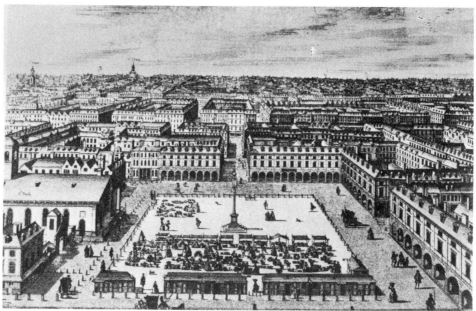

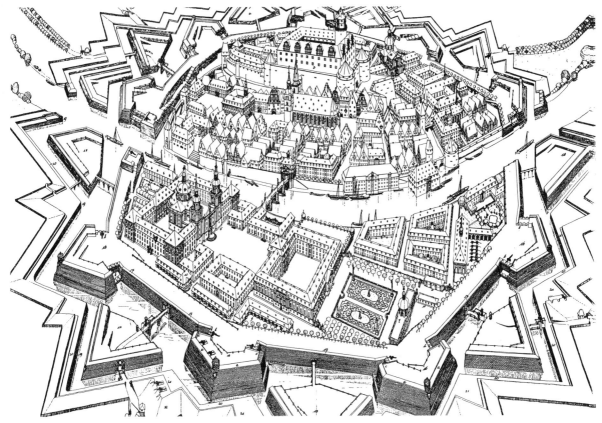

17

18: This drawing, the last in Karl Gruber's series, shows what had happened to his hypothetical German city between 1580 and 1750. Not only has the technology of the fortifications greatly increased in response to the use of cannons, but the city's organization and profile have changed. Now the city is much more regular, organized around squares and courtyards; and the spiky medieval silhouette has been replaced by the broad, symmetrical masses of the Baroque.

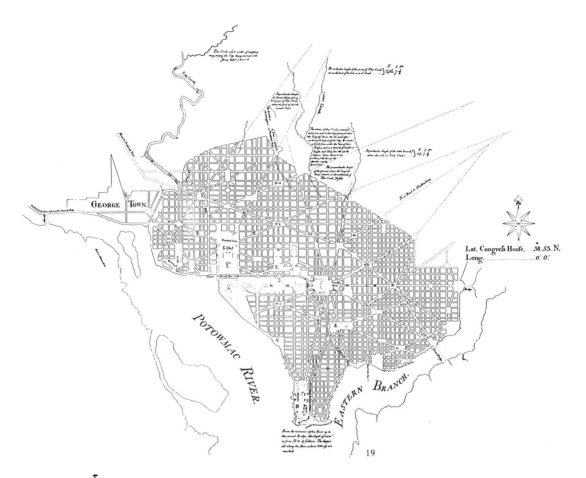

GEORGE TOWN.

POTOWMAC RIVER.

EASTERN BRANCH.

Lat. Congress House, 38. 53. N.
Long. .... 0. 0.

19

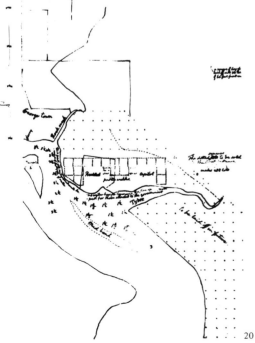

19: Andrew Ellicott's drawing of Pierre Charles L'Enfant's plan for Washington, D.C. The unfinished portions of the drawing reflect L'Enfant's dispute with the commissioners. L'Enfant was dismissed before he could complete the designs for the precincts around the White House and the Capitol. Thomas Jefferson had suggested a grid plan, in a sketch, 20, that resembled Richmond's city plan.

20

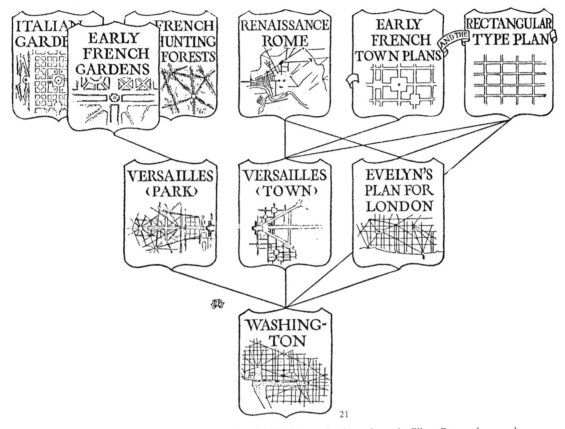

ITALIAN GARDENS · EARLY FRENCH GARDENS · FRENCH HUNTING FORESTS · RENAISSANCE ROME · EARLY FRENCH TOWN PLANS · AND THE · RECTANGULAR TYPE PLAN

VERSAILLES (PARK) · VERSAILLES (TOWN) · EVELYN'S PLAN FOR LONDON

WASHINGTON

21

21: The genealogy of L'Enfant's design ideas for Washington has been drawn by Elbert Peets, who traced influences that may well have gone into L'Enfant's thinking. Yet L'Enfant's plan was highly innovative, and a bold response to the scope and significance of the commission to design the capital city of a new republic.

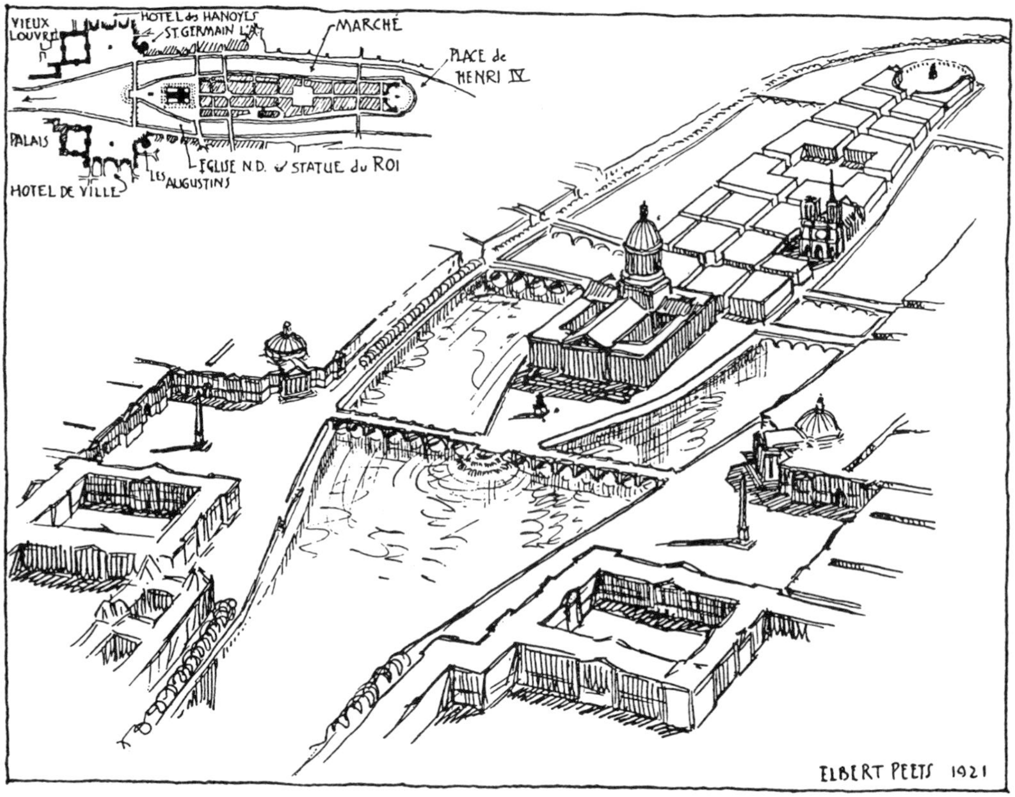

VIEUX LOUVRE
HOTEL des HANOYES
ST. GERMAIN L'A.
MARCHÉ
PLACE de HENRI IV
PALAIS
EGLISE N.D. & STATUE du ROI
LES AUGUSTINS
HOTEL DE VILLE
ELBERT PEETS 1921

22

22: Elbert Peets's projection of Pierre Patte's design for the heart of Paris that Patte published as a plan in 1765.

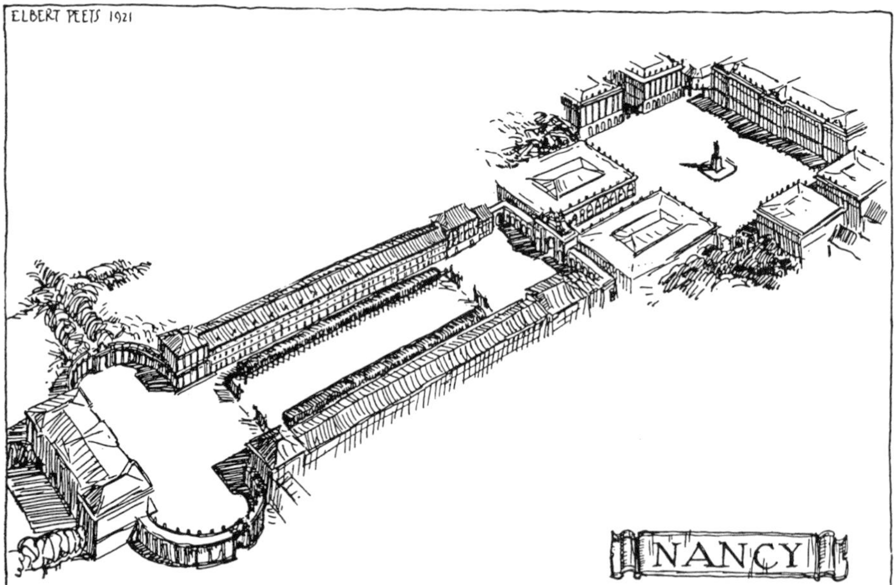

ELBERT PEETS 1921
NANCY

23

23: Another drawing by Elbert Peets, of the sequence of public spaces in Nancy, designed in the 1750s by Emmanuel Héré de Corny.

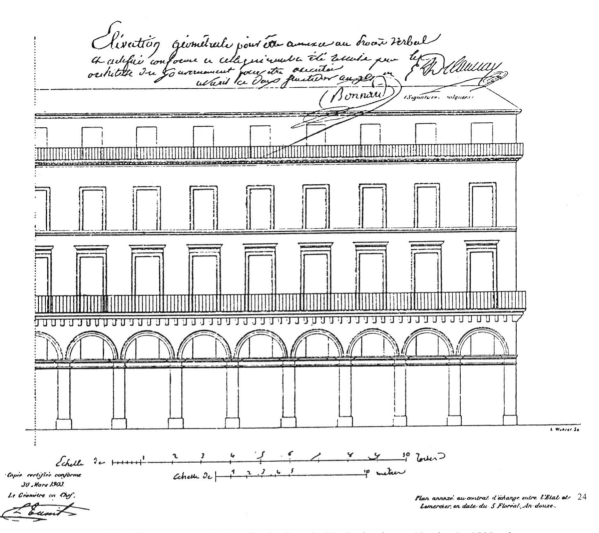

24: The official design control drawing for the Rue de Rivoli, dated year 12—that is, 1805, when Napoleon was emperor in the twelfth year after the French Revolution. The modular, uninflected design of these continuous facades reflects the more pragmatic and scientific attitude toward architecture of the early nineteenth century.

25: The Royal Crescent at Bath, like Washington, D.C., sets a geometric building organization off against an open vista of the natural landscape. The scale of the development is comparable to Nancy, but the buildings were realized incrementally in response to real estate demand rather than a royal program. The viewpoint of the sketch shown, when compared with the drawing of the quadrant of John Nash's Regent Street, 26, suggests that the architectural concept for the Quadrant is that of the Royal Crescent turned inside out. The map of the portions of Edinburgh constructed from the mid 1750s onward, 27, shows how the innovations of the Woods at Bath and of Nash in London created a new vernacular of city design. The relatively uniform architecture of the Regent Street quadrant was established by Nash through example and negotiation, the same means needed to create the route of the street itself, 29.

25

26

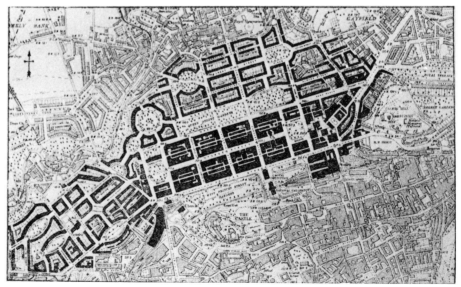

27

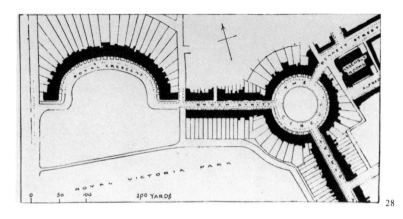

28

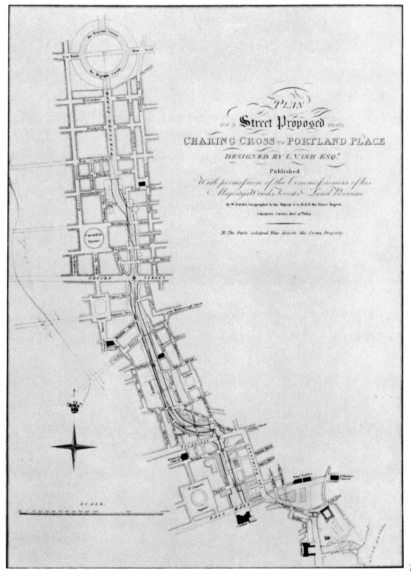

29

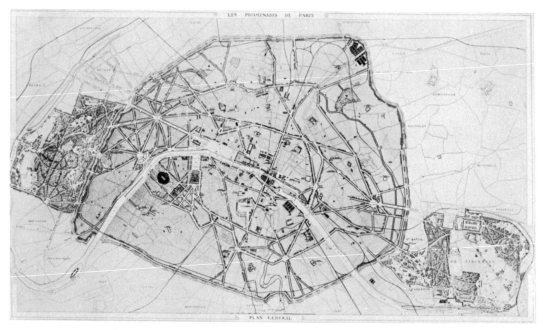

30: This map from Alphand's *Les Promenades de Paris* shows the parks and boulevards initiated while Baron Haussmann was Prefect of the Seine during the reign of Napoleon III. The narrow, dark lines leading into the city are railroads; many of the new streets were needed to connect the railway terminals to traditional central destinations.

31: The boulevards created by Haussmann had a uniformity of architecture that was implied in earlier concepts of long, straight streets, had already been constructed on the Rue de Rivoli, but had not been realized before on such an extensive scale. Part of the uniformity of height was imposed by the maximum distance that people would walk up stairs, but conformity to the overall design was enforced by codes.

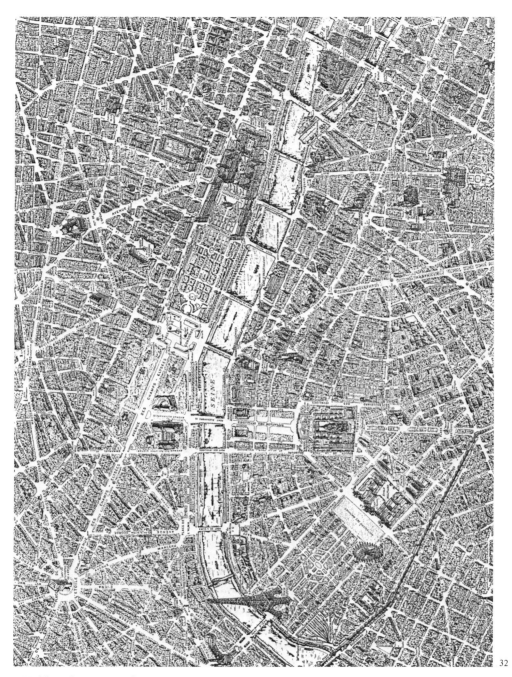

31

32

32: The urban texture of Paris—straight streets, cut through older neighborhoods with a more irregular pattern—is Haussmann's creation.

33: The lagoon at the 1893 World's Columbian Exposition in Chicago seen by moonlight. An idealized, instantaneous architectural heritage carried out in plaster, it proved to be a great influence over what people thought cities should be.

34: The McMillan Commission plan for Washington, D.C., for which Daniel Burnham, Charles F. McKim and Frederick L. Olmsted, Jr., were the designers, reclaimed much of the spirit of the L'Enfant plan but closed the axes that L'Enfant had left open to the natural landscape. McKim was to make a similar amendment to Jefferson's University of Virginia campus.

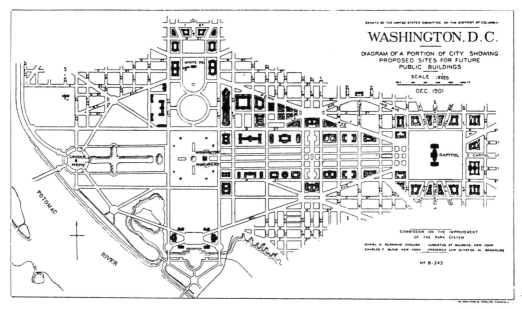

35

35, 36, 37: Daniel Burnham and Edward H. Bennett's *Plan of Chicago* of 1909 attempted to transfer Haussmann's boulevards and their accompanying uniform building height and coordinated architecture to Chicago. Although the plan proved an effective means of securing major road, railway and park improvements, the architectural continuity that had been created in Paris could not be transferred. The plan acknowledged the tall, steel-framed elevator building that had come into use since Haussmann's time, but there was no mechanism to control the shape, size and location of office, hotel and apartment towers to create the uniformity shown in the drawings. Above, an elevation of the civic center; below, proposed treatment of the intersection of the three branches of the Chicago River.

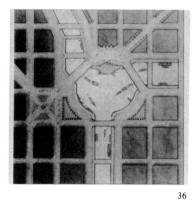

36

37

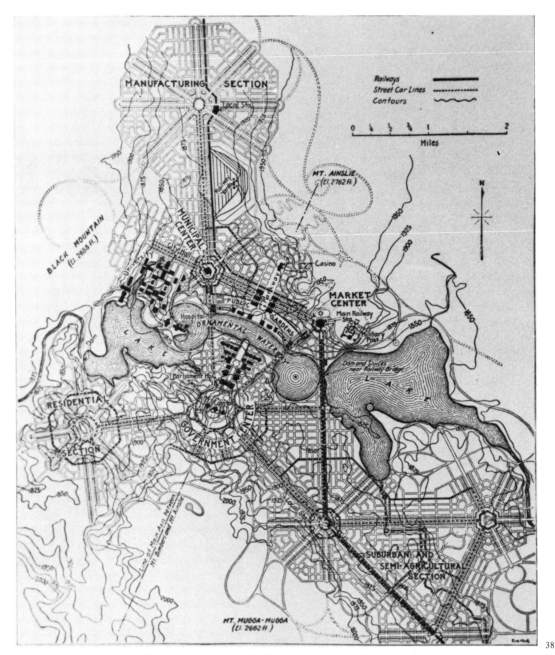

38: Walter Burley Griffin and Marion Mahony Griffin's winning competition design for Canberra, the new capital of Australia, was selected in 1912. Canberra is designed at garden-city densities but has a monumental, geometric organization that is based on the topography.

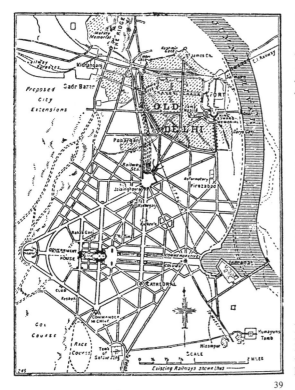

39: The Griffins' design was available to Edwin Lutyens, Herbert Baker and other members of the Delhi Town Planning Committee, who by the end of March 1913 completed a design essentially like the one shown in this illustration. Like Canberra, New Delhi is very much a garden city and it has some strong resemblances to the geometric organization of the Griffins' design.

40, 41: The main avenue approaching the central monumental building group in New Delhi was the subject of a famous controversy between Lutyens and Baker. Lutyens misunderstood a section drawing by Baker and approved the design without realizing that the dominance of the viceroy's house, which he was designing, would disappear as the road passed between the secretariats designed by Baker. These old photographs show the viceroy's house almost vanishing as the road passes between the secretariats.

42: Albert Speer's plan for the monumental center of Berlin, prepared with much consultation with Adolf Hitler, is in many respects not that different from monumental boulevards planned in other capitals. Only the great hall and triumphal arch betray underlying megalomania.

39

40

41

42

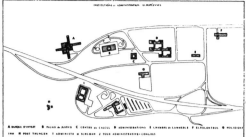

43, 44, 45: Albert Speer's architecture has been championed in recent years by Leon Krier, who has been developing a series of projects for city designs that essentially go back to the constituent elements of cities as they were before the automobile and the tall building. The project shown here takes Krier's native city of Luxembourg and imposes a new structure of squares, boulevards and monuments, designed to assimilate existing buildings into a new overall pattern.

43

44

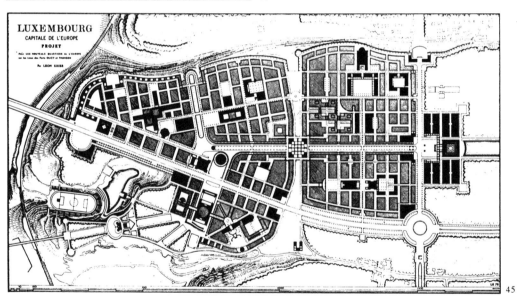

45

46: Krier's architectural ideas are less antiquarian than his style of presentation makes them appear. The building with the portico has a strong resemblance to Le Corbusier's design for the high court at Chandigarh.

46

47: Leon Krier's older brother, Rob Krier, has also been experimenting with city designs that return to urban organization as it was before the tall building. He has been able to take modern small apartments and fit them within the kinds of building that have traditionally lined European boulevards.

48

48, 49: Ricardo Bofill has been pursuing a different approach to reconciling tall modern buildings with traditional monumental city designs. He inflates the scale of column and arch, or courtyard and exedra, until they are the size of modern apartment towers.

The Garden City and Garden Suburb

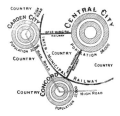

Ebenezer Howard was not an architect or a planner but a shorthand reporter in the London courts. In 1898 he published a book originally called *To-morrow a Peaceful Path to Real Reform,* but better known by its later title, *Garden Cities of To-morrow.* This short, simply written volume has had a profound effect on the design of cities.

Howard had been educated in country schools, and his first choice of a career had been to emigrate to the American frontier and become a farmer in Iowa, but he had learned from his experience that love of rural life was not enough; farming was not for him. He had also lived in Chicago from 1872 to 1876, while the city was rebuilding after the great fire. There he not only learned the shorthand that would support him for the rest of his life, but he lived in a place whose social structure was open, where people with innovative ideas could expect to get them accepted and to become successful themselves, a very different atmosphere from the stultifying class structure of England at the time.

Howard returned to a London that was in the midst of industrialization, and where Victorian, laissez-faire capitalism was at its strongest. Two views of Fleet Street looking up Ludgate Hill give some idea of what was happening. The first scene, drawn in 1827 for *London in the 19th Century,* shows a city that is still preindustrial and, allowing for the fact that the artist has left out the horse manure and the flies, possesses real charm. Gustave Doré's drawing of almost the same view in 1872 for *London, A Pilgrimage* shows the pollution and traffic congestion of the modern world. Other Doré drawings from the same book document the unspeakable conditions of the poor and the down-and-out, as well as the crowded but opulent life of the rich.

While some social reforms had taken place by the 1890s, extreme poverty, unsanitary housing and overcrowding still characterized much of London. Life was not much better in the countryside, where a prolonged agricultural depression was driving farmers off the land and reducing land prices.

Howard had an inventive mind, and had devised several improvements for typewriters and other machinery used in his office. He began to apply this inventiveness to the problems of society after reading Edward Bellamy's *Looking Backward,* which he obtained soon after it had been published in the United States, in 1888. Bellamy's novel described Boston in the year 2000 as a city where cooperation was the mainspring of society, and told of the stages by which this utopia had been brought about. Howard was so enthusiastic about the book that he immediately arranged to have it published in England, guaranteeing the sale of one hundred copies himself.

As he walked to and from the law courts through the crowds and smoke of London, Howard began to devise a new kind of city that would bring more life to rural areas, and would combine the beauty and healthfulness of the countryside with work in a modern office or industry, opportunities which at that time could be found only in a crowded, unhealthful metropolis.

The more Howard thought about *Looking Backward,* the more authoritarian and mechanistic he found its vision; and the more concerned he became that Bellamy had not thought enough about how society could make a gradual transition to a new way of life. He began to read other reformers—particularly about concepts of colonization, centralization of land ownership and model communities—before coming to his own formulation.

The book that explains his proposal is a model of clearheaded exposition. Howard begins by asking the reader to imagine that a six-thousand-acre agricultural estate has been purchased by issuing bonds secured with a mortgage on the property. This property is owned by a trust, which builds a community for thirty thousand people on one sixth of the land, leaving the rest to continue in agriculture.

At the center of the new city are the public institutions that serve the whole community: the town hall, the art gallery, theater, library, concert hall and hospital. These are surrounded by a park, which is flanked by what Howard calls the Crystal Palace and we would call a shopping center. All the shops of the city are contained in this glass-roofed building, which has a winter garden (the equivalent of the enclosed mall) as an added attraction. Around the center are the residential districts of the city, which provide building lots of different sizes for the modest or the opulent. At the perimeter are the factories, served by a circular railway siding. Beyond the factories the whole community is surrounded by rural land, which is to remain that way perpetually.

Howard knew that the railroad had made many rural areas immediately accessible to the existing network of cities and had changed the old reasons for city location. Population could be shifted to what had been remote agricultural sites if the right transportation was provided.

One of the most profitable aspects of real-estate development has always been the conversion of land from rural to urban uses. The real-estate developer ordinarily withdraws that profit from the community. Howard proposed instead to finance the development of the new city with the proceeds of the factory and house sites, and he drew up trial balance sheets to illustrate the feasibility of this development concept.

But Howard was not content to describe in outline how his proposed community might work. He was determined to include enough detail to convince any skeptic. He discusses the economics of the agricultural land, pointing out that the proximity of the new community would make market gardening and dairies feasible, and give local residents a price advantage because there would be only small shipping and distribution costs. He makes sure the reader understands that the monthly payments home-owners would have to make for land and city services would be well within their budget. He also discusses how the municipality would be staffed, and how the services could be provided and community debt retired within the amount of income to be expected.

Howard was also determined that no one should take him for an impractical utopian. He makes it clear that everything he imagines could be accomplished by the common business practices of the time in which he lived. If farmers preferred growing wheat to market gardens, fine; but it was likely that some farmers would plant vegetables because of their proximity to a good market. The factories that took sites in the new community would be ordinary factories, and the garden city corporation would have no control over them, beyond seeing that they observed some health and building regulations.

Howard then looks beyond the success of the first community to imagine what should happen when growth pressures begin to be felt. Instead of the community expanding, it should hive off a second garden city beyond the agricultural belt. Howard includes an illustration of Colonel William Light's 1836 plan for Adelaide, Australia, to show how this growth should take place. Colonel Light planned a belt of parkland all around the city of Adelaide, separating it from its suburbs, particularly from the original suburb of North Adelaide, which was also surrounded by parkland.

But this type of growth could not take place indefinitely without the assistance of the government, and Howard was confident that government would inevitably play a leading role in establishing garden cities. He reasoned by analogy to the establishment of the railroads, whose rights-of-way were at first acquired by negotiation. As the railway network became larger and of vital importance to the country, the government intervened to help railway companies acquire their routes.

What would become of London and other existing industrial cities after large numbers of the new garden communities had been built? Howard predicted that the population of the old cities would thin out until eventually they would have to be reorganized because they could no longer pay their debts. Property values would fall, and the remaining people would be able to move into the best houses, leaving the slums to be torn down and replaced by gardens.

Howard was thus advocating nothing less than the total reorganization of the entire country as something quite feasible and practical, in fact almost inevitable. His belief in the possibility of immediate constructive change was distinctly un-English: it was the confidence born of life on the American frontier.

Howard's book was not greeted with acclaim when it was published. Even the reformist Fabian Society was dismissive, the review in their newspaper stating that Howard's plans might have been adopted "if they had been submitted to the Romans when they conquered Britain."

But Howard was a tireless worker, and although he was an unpretentious person, he was an effective public speaker. Eight months after his book was published, Howard succeeded in forming a Garden City Association, promoting it by making alliances with other reform groups whose aims would be assisted by garden cities. Many of the earliest members of the association were important figures in the Land Nationalisation Society. Other influential backers were prominent lawyers who knew and respected Howard from his work in the courts. The most effective of these legal friends was Ralph Neville, who became chairman of the Garden City Association and helped Howard bring into it two important philanthropists who had supported model industrial villages, George Cadbury and W. H. Lever.

In 1901 and 1902 the Garden City Association held annual conferences: the first in Bournville, the model company town of the Cadbury chocolate company, and the second at Port Sunlight, the model town built by the Lever Brothers soap company. The first conference drew three hundred attendees, the second over a thousand. That year Howard's book was reissued under its new title, *Garden Cities of To-morrow,* and a company was set up to acquire a site for a prototype.

During 1903 over 3,800 acres were assembled at Letchworth, near the railway junction at Hitchin in Hertfordshire, and a company was formed to purchase the land and develop the new community. The groundbreaking was held on October 9, 1903.

For the design of the new community the directors selected Raymond Unwin and his brother-in-law and architectural partner, Barry Parker. Unwin at that time was forty, Parker thirty-six. They were members of the Garden City Association and had just designed a model village on garden-city principles at Earswick, near York. Now they had an opportunity to give definitive physical form to the garden city itself.

Howard, of course, had his own ideas about what a garden city should be like, although he was careful to label the illustrations that he drew for his book: "Diagram only, plans can not be drawn until site selected." All Howard's design ideas were based on concepts of cooperative action and ownership, in which he had been deeply influenced by reading Edward Bellamy's *Looking Backward.* Howard says in his book that his concept of ideal city size was derived in part from James S. Buckingham's Victoria, a model town for 25,000 described in his *National Evils and Practical Remedies.* Buckingham's designs for Victoria resemble Howard's diagrams, a rigidly symmetrical concentric plan. Buckingham, who envisioned a centrally controlled society, may well have meant his design literally. Howard understood that the workings of topography and free enterprise would produce something a great deal less organized. We also know that Howard was interested in Adelaide as a model for planned city growth, because he includes a map of it in his book, and he has to have been well aware of Nash's Regent's Park in London. The original design for Regent's Park, with its circular central element surrounded by park, has a strong resemblance to Howard's diagrams.

Unwin and Parker brought to their design of the garden city the already well-established concepts of the garden suburb and the model village, which in turn were a synthesis of two important design and planning concepts: the picturesque English gardening tradition with its artfully artificial landscape that was developed during the eighteenth century, and the conveniently planned cottage or villa with irregular and picturesque massing, also a late-eighteenth-century invention.

Picturesque design was, as its name suggests, closely related to landscape painting of the Northern European Renaissance, where the perspective vanishing point is concealed, and recession into the distance is defined by the diminishing size of overlapping natural elements like trees and hillsides. Serlio's "Satyric Scene" from his architectural treatise of 1537 shows that this type of composition was understood in Renaissance Italy contemporaneously with the strict perspective grids that outlined ideal cities. Serlio's drawing also documents the connection between this type of artistic composition and stage scenery, where the landscape shown on a backdrop is given dimensional reality by flats of trees, the largest at the proscenium and diminishing sizes placed to frame the backdrop.

British landowners who collected landscape paintings, and learned to make sketches from carefully chosen picturesque vantage points, returned from the grand tour with a desire to create picturesque landscapes out of their own estates. They also created ruins and villas to give their landscapes incident, after the manner of Poussin and Claude.

In addition, there are clear parallels between picturesque English gardens and Chinese or Japanese landscape gardening. Information about Chinese gardens was available in eighteenth-century England through travelers' reports and drawings.

Lord Burlington's garden at Chiswick is an early example. William Kent, who worked with Lord Burlington on the latter stages of Chiswick, was also one of the designers of Stowe, where Capability Brown was the head gardener. Brown went on to become one of the leading practitioners of this type of gardening. Vistas were laid out from the house, framed by trees in the foreground and by artfully placed clumps of trees or small buildings in the middle distance, and then carefully graduated plantings framed distant views. Walks were laid out through woods and fields, with prospects designed to be appreciated at intervals, where there would be benches or a garden pavilion to allow leisurely contemplation of the picture created.

Richard Payne Knight, an architect and critic, criticized Brown's landscapes as overly domesticated. In that truly eighteenth-century mode of discourse the didactic poem, Knight put forward the virtues of a more naturalistic landscape design. Humphrey Repton, a contemporary of Knight's and a generation younger than Brown, was a landscape architect whose work came closer to Knight's prescriptions. Repton created landscapes that, while they are as artificial as Brown's, look far wilder and more like undisturbed nature.

Garden designers like Brown and Repton were aided by the enclosure movement, in which large landlords were displacing tenant farmers and smallholders in order to create more grazing land for sheep. Because of the demand for cloth fostered by the spinning and weaving machines invented during the late eighteenth century, sheep raising had become more profitable than farming.

As rural villages became less economic, it was possible to edit them as well, and make them part of the landscape ensemble. There were many late-eighteenth-century and early-nineteenth-century pattern books for rural cottages, which, because they were part of the composition to be seen from the drawing-room window of a great estate, had to have more style than the genuine hovels of a rural laborer.

The rich began to acquire a taste for elaborate rural simplicity themselves, the most extreme example perhaps being the English garden and make-believe farm that Marie Antoinette had constructed on the grounds at Versailles.

John Nash was a most important figure in relating the picturesque design of large estates to the new city-design problems of the early nineteenth century. Nash's design for Cronkhill in Shropshire, for the steward of a great estate, foreshadowed the houses that would be drawn in architectural pattern books all during the nineteenth century, houses that united the picturesque composition of the rural cottage with the large, elegant rooms suitable for the suburban houses of the new merchant class, for vicars of rural parishes and for others who wished to sustain an elegant way of life though lacking the resources of the traditional great estate.

In 1810 Nash designed Blaise Hamlet, a group of charity houses on the estate of a wealthy banker. Instead of ranging the houses in neat rows, Nash grouped them around a green, positioned to define a foreground, a middle distance and a background, as in picturesque landscape composition. The design of the individual cottages anticipates the "stockbroker's Tudor" that was to become a staple of later suburbia.

A third important innovation by Nash is the design of Regent's Park, which unites townhouse development with a picturesque park on the scale of a great estate, and, had it been developed as originally planned, would have included about fifty picturesque villas integrated into the landscape. On the northeastern edge of the Regent's Park development were Park Village East and West, split by the Regent's Canal. The rows of houses, each house different, were again anticipations of later garden suburbs.

Most of the early picturesque villas in suburbs occupied rectangular plots on conventional streets. Birkenhead Park near Liverpool, designed by Joseph Paxton in 1844, creates a picturesque setting that was meant to provide preferred sites for suburban villas as well as row houses in the Regent's Park manner. Paxton had been the designer, in the late 1830s, of the picturesque model village Edensor, for the employees of the Duke of Devonshire's Chatsworth estate. Paxton's work was to prove influential in the development of the garden suburb in the United States. Birkenhead Park was visited and praised by Frederick Law Olmsted, and Edensor by Andrew Jackson Downing, who was impressed by both the site plan and the varied architecture of the individual houses.

Llewellyn Park in what is now West Orange, New Jersey, seems to represent the first complete synthesis of English garden design, and a village-like composition of elegant, but relatively small and convenient, houses into a garden suburb. Laid out by Alexander Jackson Davis in 1853, the streets are like the garden walks of an English estate. The houses were influenced by Davis's friend Andrew Jackson Downing's *Architecture of Country Houses,* which set down plans for the new type of informally arranged rural gentleman's house that had been developed in England. As at the Park Villages in Regent's Park or at Edensor, each house had a different type of architecture.

The house lots at Llewellyn Park, or at Riverside, the Chicago suburb laid out by Frederick Law Olmsted in 1869, are small compared with country estates and farms, but large enough that each house is seen to be separate from its neighbors. Walter Creese, in his book *The Search for Environment,* suggests that Ebenezer Howard may have seen Riverside while he was living in Chicago, and Creese also speculates that Howard might have been aware that Chicago before the fire had been known as the "Garden City," because of its tree-lined streets and well-cared-for yards.

Raymond Unwin and Barry Parker were probably unfamiliar with American garden suburbs when they began the design of Letchworth. Their immediate design context was the revival of vernacular architecture that took place in the latter part of the nineteenth century—usually called the Queen Anne style—despite the much broader frame of reference of most of the architecture during this period. The important work of town planning during the Queen Anne revival was Bedford Park, a garden suburb of London. A community that attracted upper-middle-class intellectuals, it was developed by Jonathan Carr, a member of an artistic and intellectual family, and its basic architectural character was established by Richard Norman Shaw, the architect who was probably most important in creating the vernacular revival. Unlike the designers of earlier suburbs, where each separate villa had its own architectural character, Shaw and the other architects who built at Bedford Park tried to create a unified environment, a village; but a village composed of commodious upper-middle-class dwellings. Other major concentrations of Queen Anne houses are to be found at Oxford and Cambridge, confirming that the Queen Anne mixture of relative architectural informality with honest expression of materials like brick and wood had a strong appeal to intellectuals.

Another major use of Queen Anne was in houses for the model villages constructed by enlightened manufacturers, such as Bournville and Port Sunlight. Parker and Unwin's first major commission had been a model village, New Earswick, near York, for the Rowntree Chocolate Trust. Parker and Unwin's work at Earswick had been influenced by the simplified cottage architecture of Charles F. A. Voysey, and they had their own strong interest in cottage improvement. They had recently published two books—*The Art of Building a Home* and *Cottage Plans and Common Sense*

—which emphasized the traditional values of the English village and advocated getting rid of wasteful snobbish elements, like the front parlor in small houses, in favor of larger rooms and convenient open plans. So it was this reformist interest in improving the architectural vernacular and restoring the virtues of village life that Unwin and Parker brought to the Letchworth commission, plus a general awareness of the British tradition of picturesque design.

Unwin and Parker's plan for Letchworth can be thought of as divided into four quadrants by the railway, which runs roughly east-west, and a main street, called Norton Way, which runs from south to north. The town square, situated on high and level ground, is located in the southwest quadrant. A monumental boulevard, Broadway, connects the town square to the place in front of the railway station and also forms the centerpiece of the residential district extending away from the town square to the southwest. The southeast quadrant contains many of the industrial sites, grouped around railway sidings, and neighborhoods of relatively modest attached houses. The shopping district lies between the station and Norton Way, on the south side of the railroad. The northeast quadrant has more factory sites along the railroad and development grouped around the previously existing village of Norton. The northwest quadrant, the last to be developed, contains Norton Common, a seventy-acre park preserve, and additional sites for light industry along the railroad.

The site plan shows a synthesis of formal and informal design concepts, with the group of straight streets leading to the town square balanced by an overall road network that is informal, but not winding and deliberately picturesque. The groups of houses and cottages, however, are artfully arranged to form architectural spaces, and were planned to create architecturally related groups, not a variety of different styles. Unwin and Parker placed the community athwart the railroad, rather than tangential to it, as Howard's diagram showed. Site design decisions were made on the basis of topography, prevailing winds and existing vegetation. The industrial location on the east side of the town meant that prevailing winds would blow industrial pollution away from most residences. There is no sign of the Crystal Palace that Howard had suggested, but the main shopping street could be interpreted as representing about one eighth of the shopping district Howard had diagrammed, which was actually all a community the size of Letchworth could be expected to support.

What Unwin and Parker did for Letchworth was to give Howard's radical ideas an expression that was totally unthreatening, and that had been artfully designed to evoke traditional English villages.

Letchworth is important because it gave the first physical form to Howard's vision of a new social order, but Raymond Unwin and Barry Parker's next commission, in 1905, to develop the site plan for Hampstead Garden Suburb was to have a far wider influence on the design of cities. Their client was Henrietta Barnett, a social reformer who was married to Canon S. A. Barnett, a pioneer in the settlement-house movement. The site, in the Golders Green section of London north of Hampstead Heath, was about to become accessible as a result of the extension of an underground rapid transit line, completed in 1907.

The social program was to create a community open to a wide range of different incomes, with the hope that eventually proximity would help break down class barriers; the community was also to be made as close to an ideal environment as possible, embodying, as Howard had suggested, the advantages of both town and country.

However, Hampstead was to be a suburb, an extension of London, and thus contrary to Howard's basic theory that the growth that was going into the extension of the metropolis should be channeled into separate garden cities instead. Unwin and Parker's acceptance of this commission has often been described as something very like an act of disloyalty to the garden-city movement, but the garden suburb was actually a well-established concept that could hardly be considered a heresy against Howard's much newer doctrine.

By the time Unwin and Parker began the design of Hampstead they had become aware of the theories of Camillo Sitte and had begun reading *Der Städtebau,* the German periodical that published the work of Sitte and like-minded city designers and was a primary force in creating city planning as a professional discipline. Raymond Unwin's *Town Planning in Practice,* published in 1909, contains the first serious treatment of Sitte's theories in English.

Sitte's approach was to look not at the logic of plans but at what the viewer would actually see walking near the buildings, and then to codify principles based on comparative experience. The perception of the city as a succession of changing viewpoints is very close to the picturesque aesthetic of English garden design. Sitte believed that many monumental plazas were far too large; and while important public buildings should keep their prominent position, they should be attached to the other buildings that form the wall of a plaza, or be closely related to them. In this way, space would be contained and not merely implied in plan.

Reading Sitte and *Der Städtebau* led Unwin and Parker to look at some of the examples of city design continually referred to in German practice. The exceptionally well-preserved medieval city of Rothenburg seems to have been of particular interest, judging from the illustrations selected by Unwin for his book.

Another important influence on the design of Hampstead Garden Suburb was the association of Edwin Lutyens with the plan and Lutyens's work as architect of some of the principal buildings. Lutyens was a master of scenographic architectural effects, and far more sophisticated than Unwin and Parker about what was needed to create a strong architectural design. Lutyens, however, was more inclined than Unwin and Parker to put architecture ahead of social objectives. As the architect for the central building group at Hampstead, Lutyens got into a tremendous struggle with Henrietta Barnett and the board of directors over the height and scale of the central buildings—Lutyens seeking to give the two churches architectural dominance over the community, the board feeling that such prominence was inappropriate. The board did get Lutyens to modify his designs. From an architectural standpoint, Lutyens was probably right, as the central district is not immediately visible from many parts of Hampstead, so that the overall composition loses legibility. However, dominance of the two central churches would have misstated the nature of the community; it was not a medieval village.

The site plan of Hampstead is much tighter than that of Letchworth and the architectural grouping far stronger. The key difference is the use at Hampstead of cul-de-sac streets. The cul-de-sac had been made illegal under building bylaws because of its abuse in the early urban slum districts. It required an act of Parliament to use the cul-de-sac at Hampstead.

The cul-de-sac creates a hierarchy of streets, by distinguishing between streets needed purely for access to individual dwellings and streets that carried traffic. It encouraged the grouping of buildings into courtyards, and Unwin and Parker arranged whole districts in a pattern of alternating streets and gardens so that each house had both a street and a garden view. This concept was later to be more fully developed at Radburn by Henry Wright and Clarence Stein.

Ebenezer Howard's writings and tireless promotional efforts made the concept of the garden city internationally known, but the image of the garden city was established by Unwin and Parker, and it is much more the image of Hampstead Garden Suburb than it is of Letchworth. Hampstead was more accessible; it had a superior site plan, which created architecturally defined spaces; and with its greater range of incomes, it had far more distinguished architecture—including the central grouping of buildings by Edwin Lutyens, Waterlow Court by M. H. Baillie Scott, and courtyard groups by Unwin and Parker themselves.

It was the image of Hampstead that had an immediate effect on the design of suburbs almost everywhere, while it would take another generation for Howard's basic planning concepts to begin to receive a similar degree of acceptance.

While Unwin and Parker were learning from Camillo Sitte and *Der Städtebau,* their work was becoming influential in the German-speaking world because it was included in the book entitled *Das Englische Haus* (1905), by Hermann Muthesius. Muthesius had been a cultural attaché in the German embassy in London, and had made a serious study of English domestic architecture.

A German Garden City Association was founded in 1908 to construct a garden city at Hellerau, near Dresden. Hellerau was in some ways a company town for the workers in the Dresden Craft Workshops, owned by the enlightened furniture manufacturer Karl Schmidt. The town was run independently, however, and contained a district of relatively large houses as well as the attached cottages for workers, all designed in a picturesque German village style by Richard Riemerschmid. Hellerau, like Hampstead, became a center for advanced social thought, and the site of Émile Jaques Dalcroze's famous school.

The Falkenberg district of Berlin, designed by Bruno Taut in 1912, was a much more ambitious garden suburb, sponsored by cooperative housing associations. It was designed in a more urbane style than Hellerau, with Hampstead-like cul-de-sacs, row houses and even a crescent. The initial buildings, begun just before the First World War, resembled the restrained architectural style of the early nineteenth century.

The planned suburb of Margaretenhöhe, near Essen, designed by Georg Metzendorf in 1912, one of a series of model company towns for workers in the Krupp steel and munitions plants, clearly shows the influence of Unwin and Parker's planning. So, interestingly enough, does contemporary work by Camillo Sitte himself, such as his plan for Marienberg. Other important early examples of garden suburbs created under the influence of Hampstead include Munkkiniemi-Haaga outside Helsinki, designed by Eliel Saarinen in 1916; Ulleval, near Oslo, by Oscar Hoff and Harald Hals, designed in 1918; and the garden suburbs of Stockholm.

The influence of Letchworth and Hampstead Garden Suburb was seen almost immediately in the United States at Forest Hills Gardens, a model suburb of New York City developed, beginning in 1909, at the instigation of the Russell Sage Foundation. The landscape architect who designed the parks and curving street system was Frederick Law Olmsted, Jr.; Grosvenor Atterbury established the character of the architecture and designed the important buildings and groups of houses. Although many of the houses at Forest Hills Gardens are of poured reinforced concrete, which was still an experimental building material in 1909, they are covered in brick, stone or stucco in a free interpretation of the Tudor style, more of a single period than the Queen Anne that had characterized Bedford Park. As the informal, comfortable house, suitable for the upper-middle-class life, had been an English invention, an English country-house style often seemed to be the appropriate symbol of these qualities. Forest Hills Gardens, like Hampstead, was designed for a mix of incomes, with apartment houses in the town center and along the railroad tracks, attached houses, and individual houses of various sizes.

In designing Forest Hills Gardens the Olmsted firm could also draw on its experience at the planned suburb of Roland Park, north of Baltimore, in the late 1890s; but where Roland Park depended for its design on the arrangement of its streets, Forest Hills Gardens, like Hampstead, created real architectural spaces, particularly in Atterbury's design for the center near the railroad station and for housing groups. Forest Hills Gardens and Hampstead can be seen to have influenced the groups of houses around courtyards constructed in suburbs like Germantown and Chestnut Hill, Pennsylvania, about the time of the First World War and the design for the town center of Lake Forest, Illinois, by Howard Van Doren Shaw, dating from 1916. Lake Forest is otherwise a garden suburb of the older type, laid out in the mid-nineteenth century as a loose composition of winding streets and large house lots.

American company towns influenced by English examples include Kohler, Wisconsin, laid out by the Olmsted firm in 1913, and Tyrone, New Mexico. The latter—begun in 1915, never completed, and ultimately demolished in 1967—was a brilliant translation by Bertram G. Goodhue of the Unwin-Parker concept. Instead of the English village idiom used at Forest Hills Gardens or Lake Forest, Goodhue used an architectural vocabulary based upon Spanish colonial and pueblo architecture.

In their winning design for Canberra, Australia, Walter and Marion Griffin used monumental principles of organization; but in its overall density, their plan was that of the garden city, and its use of a railway line to link population subcenters was also related to garden-city theory.

Both Griffins had worked in Oak Park for Frank Lloyd Wright, but their plan is closer to Burnham's designs for Chicago than to anything that came out of Wright's office. The three highest points on the contour map were chosen as the political, commercial and military centers and linked by long, straight avenues forming an equilateral triangle. In the valley between Parliament Hill and the other high points is a chain of lakes, with formal basins within the triangle and adjoining it. A third axis from Parliament Hill crosses the central basin, creating the familiar system of three radial axes seen at the entrance to Rome and at Versailles.

While the street system is essentially formal, based on long boulevards and radial streets around subcenters, it is carefully adjusted to the contours, and the neighborhoods are scaled for houses on individual lots.

There was strong political opposition to the selection of Griffin, a foreigner, as the planner of Canberra and to the whole idea of a new capital, which turned the victory in the competition into a bitter experience. Griffin stuck it out until 1920, doggedly mapping the street system, knowing that once it had been laid out no one would bother to do the work over again. As a result, despite many changes, the essence of the Griffin plan has been implemented.

After Forest Hills Gardens, the most significant manifestation of the influence of the garden-city concept in the United States was the design of emergency housing created as a response to the vast industrial expansion that began during the First World War.

When the United States entered the war in 1917, it was clear that unprecedented amounts of new housing would be needed to accommodate the large number of workers suddenly brought to industrial sites. Two federal agencies supported housing construction. The Housing Division of the Emergency Fleet Corporation gave loans to private companies, which built the towns; and the United States Housing Corporation built and operated units. The former completed 9,000 family dwellings plus another 7,500 small apartments and boardinghouse rooms; the latter completed 6,000 dwellings in 27 projects.

Charles Whitaker, then the editor of the *Journal of the American Institute of Architects,* campaigned to make sure that this wartime housing was designed not as temporary barracks but as permanent communities. He sent the architect Frederick L. Ackerman to England to consult with Raymond Unwin, who was in charge of the British war-housing effort and published a series of articles on British housing standards, which dealt with war housing as a permanent investment.

Frederick Law Olmsted, Jr., who had earlier volunteered to help organize the design and building of army bases for the Quartermaster Corps, was put in charge of the planning section of the United States Housing Corporation. Olmsted also wished to make sure that the American wartime housing ended up as permanent communities designed to high standards; and he was in a position to name as designers for this housing some of the best architects and planners in the United States.

George B. Post & Sons' design for Eclipse Park, in Beloit, Wisconsin —planned for the employees of Fairbanks, Morse and Company—bears a distinct resemblance to Forest Hills Gardens, although the houses were more modest. There is a town center, which acts as a gateway to the community, curving landscaped streets and a large park. Another excellent example is Kingsport, Tennessee, designed by John Nolen, an important planner and a disciple of Unwin and Parker. George B. Post & Sons designed houses and apartments for shipyard workers at Craddock, Virginia (near Hampton Roads), that were as well planned and detailed as contemporary private housing being built in well-to-do suburbs, although building dimensions and lots were smaller.

Other company towns built under these programs as garden suburbs include Westinghouse Village in South Philadelphia, Pennsylvania, whose plan by Clarence W. Brazer shows the influence of Hampstead adapted to an American vernacular; Yorkship Village, West Collingswood, New Jersey, by Electus D. Litchfield, also clearly influenced by Hampstead Garden Suburb; and Seaside and Black Rock in Bridgeport, Connecticut, planned by Arthur Shurtleff, with R. Clipston Sturgis and A. H. Hepburn as architects.

The government subsidy for workers' housing was viewed at the time as a necessary, but temporary, expedient, and the laws setting up the programs required that the housing be sold as soon as the war was over. In an introduction to a book describing these wartime housing projects, the then secretary of labor commented:

> I have found that the man who owns his own home is the least susceptible to the so-called Bolshevist doctrines and is about the last man to join in the industrial disturbances fomented by the radical agitators. Owning a home gives a man an added sense of responsibility to the national and local government that makes for the best type of citizenship.

This belief in the importance of the owner-occupied house was not shared in Europe, where governments began to subsidize housing on a large scale after the First World War. In England large amounts of subsidized housing for workers were designed to similar standards to those created at Letchworth, helped by the 1912 publication of Raymond Unwin's pamphlet *Nothing Gained by Overcrowding* and Unwin's own activities as a government official. His argument was that the conventional bylaw streets required for densities of twenty houses per acre or higher cost so much more to develop that they more than canceled the higher price of land per house at densities of twelve houses per acre.

The absorption of the Garden City Association into the more broadly based Town and Country Planning Association was symptomatic of what seemed to be happening to Ebenezer Howard's ideas in the years after the First World War. Howard, with his cheerfully optimistic temperament, remained undeterred in his belief in a future radical transformation of society, and refused to accept that the major result of his efforts to date seemed to be better-designed suburbs, not a new type of city. After all, he had turned out to be correct in predicting that a planned garden city under community ownership would be economically feasible. Howard's only miscalculation, which was serious but not fatal, was that it took much longer than he had estimated to bring the community up to a size that generated sufficient income to pay off its debts.

Pleased but not satisfied by the modest success of Letchworth, Howard began looking out for places to build a second prototype. A site near Hatfield that he had marked down as ideal before the end of the war came on the market in 1919. Howard persuaded his backers to buy it, although many of his colleagues urged him to put his energies into getting the government to incorporate new-town policies into postwar housing development, as proposed by Frederick J. Osborn in his 1918 book *New Towns After the War.* Howard did not wish to wait idly for governmental support; he preferred to continue demonstrating the virtues of garden cities by direct action. The result was Welwyn Garden City, which also was to become an established community. Welwyn would not have succeeded, however, without government loan money, made available as part of the postwar housing programs, which included a clause that permitted loans to associations created for the purpose of developing garden cities.

The design concept for Welwyn, by Louis de Soissons, is close to that of Letchworth. The monumental boulevard has more importance, and the overall site plan is somewhat more tightly organized, but the industrial district is positioned analogously to the one at Letchworth and there is a similarly informal network of winding streets. The design of housing groups is more architectural, reflecting design advances made at Hampstead, and the prevailing architectural character is a somewhat anemic neo-Georgian.

Additional planned communities were created in Britain during the interwar period on Howard-like principles, but they were constructed by major cities as part of public policies dealing with housing and overcrowding, and were not developed by an autonomous private group, as Welwyn was. Wythenshawe, near Manchester, was constructed by the city of Manchester and designed by Barry Parker (Unwin had remained in government service after the war and the partnership had been dissolved). While it was far more a one-class community of subsidized housing than Howard had advocated, and it lacked its own employment base, Wythenshawe continued the development of the garden-city concept by creating new types of housing groups and cul-de-sacs.

The London County Council began a series of what it called cottage housing estates after World War I, the largest of which were definitely on a new-town scale, but they were suburbs rather than complete communities. Beacontree, east of London, was designed by C. Topham Forrest, architect to the London County Council, in 1920. It was planned for a population of 115,000, making it far larger than other LCC cottage housing groups planned at the same period around the fringes of London. Some of these housing projects were nevertheless at new-town size, such as Downham, designed to house 30,000 people, or the St. Helier estate, for 45,000. Altogether, dwellings for some 300,000 people were developed, all designed under the direction of Forrest or his successor, E. P. Wheeler. Densities were almost always at twelve persons to the acre, there were ample reservations for open space, and the buildings were of a uniformly high architectural quality. Care was taken to create architectural groups along curving streets or around cul-de-sacs, but the uniformity of income level, density and building type inevitably produced a certain monotony.

The new-town ideal also influenced some of the subsidized housing development on the continent of Europe during the interwar period, although most of this housing, as we will see in the next chapter, was constructed in a more urban pattern. Ernst May, the city architect of Frankfurt, had worked for Unwin and Parker before the First World War and was thus thoroughly familiar with the theories of Ebenezer Howard and with the completed English garden cities and suburbs. While May and his colleagues used a modernist architectural vernacular, they gave their work a humane quality that was missing from the mechanistic efforts of many other modernists of the time. May prepared a comprehensive plan for Frankfurt, which was the context for his housing projects. He also developed new satellite communities at Romerstadt, Praunheim and Westhausen, which combined English garden-city planning principles, like curving streets and greenbelts, with German ideas about simplified architectural expression and the importance of orientation as an architectural determinant.

In the United States after the First World War, some of the best new housing took the form of model garden communities built by private companies seeking a sound, long-term investment, as well as a worthwhile social purpose.

Mariemont, east of Cincinnati, was built on land assembled by Mrs. Mary M. Emery starting in 1923. Mrs. Emery donated a park, a church and the first school buildings, but the aim of the company was to make a suitable profit while providing good-quality housing for skilled workmen and salaried office workers who would not otherwise be able to afford it. The planner was John Nolen, one of the pioneers of effective city planning in the United States, and the layout followed the now familiar garden-suburb pattern.

Sunnyside, in the New York City borough of Queens, was begun in 1924 as a model community by the limited-profit City Housing Corporation. The planners, Clarence Stein and Henry Wright, had to accept a preexisting street grid pattern, but were able to create open spaces in the interior of the blocks and, later, through-block common spaces between groups of buildings. The result was far better than the rows of identical houses on narrow lots that were the normal form of competing development. Also, through its limited-profit structure, Sunnyside, like Mariemont, was able to reach people of somewhat lower incomes than the buyers of conventional houses. There were also apartment houses, both rental and cooperative.

Sunnyside was a dress rehearsal for the City Housing Corporation's more ambitious Radburn, New Jersey, planned as the American equivalent of Letchworth or Welwyn, after consultation with Unwin and Parker, and begun in 1928. Because of the Depression, only a small portion of the community was completed in accordance with the original plan; but that plan, also provided by Clarence Stein and Henry Wright, has proved tremendously influential. Its most important feature was its greenway system, which allowed children to walk to the primary school by pathways that never crossed a street—except for one underpass below a main road. Clarence Stein used to say that the greenway and underpass system was suggested by the separation between pedestrians and vehicles in Manhattan's Central Park, but the design can also be interpreted as deriving from some very similar arrangements at Hampstead Garden Suburb and from the traditional alternation of streets and service alleys. At Radburn, all services are on cul-de-sac streets leading to clusters of houses, and what in other projects might have been an alley has become the greenway.

The concept of a neighborhood unit like the one at Radburn as a group of houses and apartments large enough to require a primary school was part of Clarence Perry's definition of a neighborhood in a 1929 essay published as part of the First Regional Plan for New York City. This plan, which was issued in installments starting in 1926, was supported by the Russell Sage Foundation, which had developed Forest Hills Gardens, where Perry, the foundation's director, lived. Not surprisingly, the theoretical drawing of a neighborhood given in the plan bears a strong resemblance to Forest Hills Gardens. The idea of neighborhoods has become such an axiomatic part of planning that one tends to forget that it was formulated by a few individuals, such as Perry, Stein and Wright, as part of the design of isolated model developments that housed only a few thousand families. In time the ideas were to feed back into the English garden-city movement and would ultimately be adopted all over the world. Barry Parker was particularly impressed by Radburn, and incorporated its redefinition of the cul-de-sac into his designs for Wythenshawe.

The coming of the New Deal in the United States seemed to create the opportunities to apply all the city-planning ideas that had been created as prototypes by privately supported developments. The Tennessee Valley Authority would offer the opportunity to do real regional planning on an unprecedented scale. New federal programs accepted the principle already established in Europe that it was up to government to supply good-quality low-income housing if the private market could not do it. Many of these programs were federal subsidies to local housing authorities, but the government also went into the housing development business itself. The Resettlement Administration, one of the many agencies established during the early days of the New Deal, was under the direction of Rexford Tugwell, who was a firm believer in Ebenezer Howard's garden-city theories. The Resettlement Administration proposed four greenbelt communities and actually constructed three of them: Greenbelt, Maryland, located about ten miles northeast of Washington; Greendale, Wisconsin, seven miles from Milwaukee; and Greenhills, Ohio, five miles north of Cincinnati.

While planned to be self-contained satellite communities on Howard's model, these towns actually ended up becoming garden suburbs. The one greenbelt town site that might successfully have attracted industry would have been Greenbrook, near New Brunswick, New Jersey, which was not built because of political opposition. Despite the actual construction of these greenbelt communities, the model had little effect on American real-estate development practice, perhaps because construction by the federal government, and the income restrictions on tenancies, made the whole greenbelt idea seem remote from normal development practice.

During the exciting early days of the New Deal, when almost any radical idea could be given a serious hearing, no one talked seriously to Frank Lloyd Wright, who was certainly understood to be a great architect, but was also well known to be a controversial and difficult personality. Wright tried to remedy this situation by preparing designs for Broadacre City, which were exhibited in 1935 at Rockefeller Center in New York City, then used by Wright as illustrations for various books and polemics, and as sources for actual building designs. Wright had already predicted, in his book *The Disappearing City,* published in 1932, that the automobile would cause a fundamental change in city design, with urbanization spreading out over the landscape. Wright welcomed this change, rejecting the modern central city as an unnatural and inhumane environment.

For Broadacre City, Wright went back to a design for a typical midwestern mile-square land segment that he had prepared in 1913, and enlarged his prototype area to four miles. Wright rejected the curving streets of English and American garden-suburb design, and proposed a much lower density: in some sections of his plan, each family would have an acre of land.

The social intentions behind Broadacre City have puzzled a number of commentators, and its ideological contradictions have been the subject of a long essay by Giorgio Ciucci. Unlike Ebenezer Howard, or Clarence Stein, Wright had no serious social agenda. If you look closely at the floor plans for Broadacre City houses, you find that many of them have one or more maid's rooms. Wright accepted society as he found it. He just wished to shape its buildings. Broadacre City is probably best understood as an advertisement. It is also, at a secondary level, an answer to Le Corbusier's Ville Contemporaine (which we will come to in the next chapter) and the more mechanistic architectural ideas of European modernism. Wright wanted to show Americans a modern city that was closely related to the American way of life. Broadacre City is a fairly accurate prediction of post–World War II suburban sprawl, particularly areas with large-lot zoning, showing that Wright understood the American public well. What he was unable to do, however, was invent a mechanism that would ensure that this type of suburban and exurban growth would follow any overall design. Thus Broadacre City itself has had very little influence. Where Wright has been enormously influential has been through the house types that he was developing for individual owners at the same time that he was working on Broadacre City. These "Usonian" houses did much to transform the typical suburban house from a miniature version of the English gentleman's residence into a dwelling that was far more open, functional and in tune with modern life.

Chatham Village in Pittsburgh, by Clarence Stein and Henry Wright with the Pittsburgh architects Ingham and Boyd, was designed in the early 1930s to be a prototype that would turn the American public away from the single-family house on an individual lot to a planned village environment similar to English garden cities and suburbs. Developed by the Buehl Foundation as a limited-profit investment, Chatham Village builds on the experience of Sunnyside and Radburn but possesses an architectural and landscaping distinction not achieved in the earlier projects. Chatham Village could have been the model for post–World War II development in the United States in terms of its cost efficiency for both buildings and land, but it did not inspire this kind of emulation.

The city-design idea that captured the admiration of the American public was the garden suburb for upper-income people that could be found on the fashionable side of almost every American city by the end of the interwar period. One of the major changes that took place in Middletown (Muncie, Indiana) between Robert and Helen Merrell Lynd's original study in 1928 and their *Middletown in Transition* study of 1937 was the growth of a fashionable suburban district and the consequent segregation of well-off citizens in their own enclave, away from the center of the community.

Whatever the negative social effects of the new garden suburbs, they frequently included elements that made them desirable environments, such as parks, curving streets and secluded cul-de-sacs. The Country Club district of Kansas City, River Oaks in Houston, and Palos Verdes and Beverly Hills in Los Angeles are well-known examples.

Dodsworth, a Sinclair Lewis character who, like George Babbitt, lived in Zenith, bought a house in one of the new suburbs,

> So far as possible, the builders kept the beauties of forest and hills and river; the roads were not to be broad straight gashes butting their way through hills, but winding byways, very inviting . . . if one could only kill off the motorists.

Ebenezer Howard died in 1928. The two garden cities Letchworth and Welwyn had reached a combined population of forty thousand by World War II. While this is success of a sort, the population of Great Britain increased enough between 1898 and 1945 to have created three hundred garden cities without changing the population of the cities that already existed. It was not until after the Second World War that Howard's satellite city formulation was widely adopted in Great Britain and Europe, and then throughout the world. The process of acceptance, however, also involved a transformation. It is not clear that Howard would have approved the planning that has been done in his name, or even have recognized the results as garden cities. Where Howard sought to disperse all social classes from cities into networks of autonomous communities, the new town has been used as a satellite for big cities, and has often become a community made up predominantly of factory workers.

Patrick Abercrombie's Greater London Plan for postwar reconstruction, published in 1944, used greenbelts and satellite towns as a way of limiting the growth of London. Government new-town policy then extended the concept to all of Britain, and something like forty of these communities are in various stages of development. Decentralization of industry laws made it possible to give each new town an economic base, in keeping with Howard's ideas; but because the new towns did not constitute the whole of urban development, they became primarily working-class communities.

In Sweden, where foresighted land acquisition policies had enabled the city of Stockholm to control its growth, much of the suburban development was channeled into planned communities like Vällingby, designed by Sven Markelius, and Farsta. The map of the Stockholm metropolitan region has a cellular appearance, with shopping centers along regional railroad corridors and higher-density growth around the stations, with feeder roads leading out to lower-density areas.

Helsinki, Finland, has also successfully channeled growth into satellite communities, some of which, like Tapiola, have attracted international attention for the high quality of the buildings.

French national planning policies have directed the growth of the Paris metropolitan region into planned satellite communities along two axes roughly parallel to the Seine north and south of Paris, with this development pattern supported by a new regional rail system.

The original garden-city image has been altered in these postwar planned communities by the introduction of elevator buildings, but curving streets and informal building arrangements have been the usual pattern for new development in previously rural areas. While most European cities have planned garden suburbs of this newer high-density type, anything like a self-contained community is rare, except in Great Britain.

In the United States there have been a few economically successful planned communities built since the Second World War. These include Reston, Virginia, near Washington; Columbia, Maryland, between Washington and Baltimore, the Woodlands north of Houston, Texas; and the Irvine Ranch development between Los Angeles and San Diego. Reston is the most self-sufficient of these communities—reluctantly, as the original plan was to connect Reston to Washington by the highway that leads to Dulles Airport. When access to that highway was denied, development was slowed down.

In the 1970s there was also a brief official flirtation with new towns as a federal policy, with government-subsidized loans provided to developers of approved planned communities. While a few of these communities, notably the Woodlands, have proved to be sound investments, most were disastrous failures. No more towns are being built under the program, and the federal government is overseeing liquidation wherever possible.

The most important difference between the city that Howard was trying to change and the modern period has turned out to be the widespread acceptance of automobiles and trucks, which have become the primary means of transportation in most cities. Howard's diagram of self-contained communities separated by greenbelts was perfectly adapted to the railroad as a means of transportation; it is not economically obvious that development should be confined to areas around station stops and along railway sidings when cars and trucks are available.

Economic viability for a planned community is also more difficult to achieve than Howard anticipated. In many cases the community has made no money for its original investors. A long-term investment strategy that is beyond the time horizons of most real-estate developers is always required. As a result, governments have been the primary backers of planned communities. Howard had foreseen a role for government in creating new towns, but he did not consider that governments might by their nature have more limited social objectives than he did. In his quietly subversive way, Howard had hoped to bring about a total transformation of society, not marginal improvements.

Howard's concept of urban expansion, on the other hand, has proved a very sound prediction. As Howard anticipated, cities have decentralized; and the economy of the older central city has become weaker as a consequence.

On the fashionable side of major metropolitan areas are miles and miles of town-country, much as Howard defined it. There are office and industrial parks, regional shopping centers and spread-out residential neighborhoods. People can live, work and shop in these districts, without entering the old downtown more than a few times a year, if at all. What is missing, of course, is the city-design structure that Howard imagined; the greenbelts and tight clusters of development so appropriate to the railroad and so difficult to achieve in the age of the automobile. The social diversity that Howard had hoped to achieve is also missing. In his scheme of things, the profits from the real-estate developments would have subsidized the homes of the lower-income members of the community.

Where the garden-city concept has been most successful has been in demonstrating that whole districts of cities can be designed in a unified way in a sympathetic relationship to the natural landscape, which is essentially an achievement of Raymond Unwin and Barry Parker and the architects and planners they influenced.

The suburb of curving streets and cul-de-sacs, where houses are built in a lawn-and-garden setting, has become standard planning practice, written into thousands of subdivision regulations.

There is also a revival of interest by real-estate developers in creating suburban development comparable in architectural interest and landscape quality to older garden suburbs that have kept their high property values and social prestige. Often these new developments are subdivisions of large estates in older suburban areas. Robert A. M. Stern, who has made himself an exponent of the virtues of the garden suburb, has now designed several suburban subdivisions for upper-income people that are very close both architecturally and scenically to the garden suburbs of the 1920s.

Thus, while Ebenezer Howard was not quite the prophet of a new social order, his advocacy and the events he helped set in motion continue to be remarkably influential.

50: London, looking up Fleet Street toward Ludgate Hill in 1827. The scene still shows a preindustrial city and, allowing for the fact that the artist has left out the horse manure and the flies, possesses real charm. 51, *Below:* Gustave Doré's drawing of almost the same view in 1872 shows the pollution and traffic congestion of the modern world.

50

51

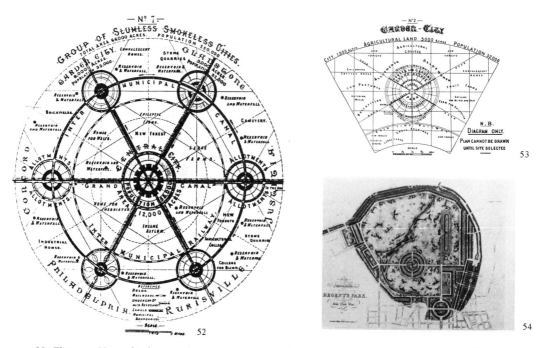

53

54

52: Ebenezer Howard's drawing shows a cluster of garden cities replacing the congested and polluted metropolis of his day; the conception is worked out in meticulous detail, 53, although Howard was careful to use the label "diagram only." The design sources for Howard's diagrams may have included John Nash's original design for Regent's Park, 54, and, 55, Joseph Paxton's Birkenhead Park, 1844, near Liverpool, which combine high-density town houses with a parklike landscape.

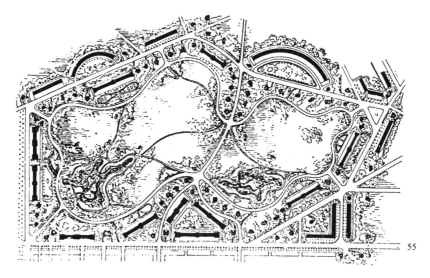

55

56: The tradition of picturesque garden and park design, which had a strong influence on Raymond Unwin and Barry Parker's plan for Howard's first garden city, is derived from Northern European landscape painting and travelers' reports of Chinese gardens. It had become a well-established vernacular, as this engraving from an early-nineteenth-century German gardening book demonstrates. Winding paths are designed to provide a series of vistas, which are sometimes framed by specially designed pavilions as well as by artfully placed landscaping.

57, 58: Picturesquely designed estates sometimes included well-composed model villages, which replaced the genuine hovels of rural laborers. Milton Abbas, by William Chambers and Capability Brown, from the late 1770s, and John Nash's Blaise Hamlet, 1811, are early examples.

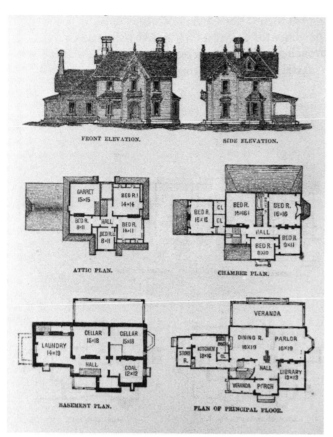

FRONT ELEVATION.   SIDE ELEVATION.

ATTIC PLAN.   CHAMBER PLAN.

BASEMENT PLAN.   PLAN OF PRINCIPAL FLOOR.

59

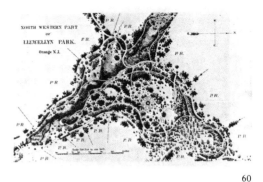

60

After the introduction of railroads, the translation of picturesque model villages or villa estates like Regent's and Birkenhead parks into picturesque suburbs happened quickly in the United States. Alexander Jackson Davis drew his plans for Llewellyn Park, New Jersey, in 1852, 60. The house by Calvert Vaux, 59, was designed for a lot in Llewellyn Park. The picturesque suburban villa could now have an appropriately picturesque setting, instead of the rectangular lots where it had usually been built until this time.

61: The plan of Riverside, a suburb of Chicago, laid out by Frederick Law Olmsted in 1869, could be the plan of a suburb laid out today, so durable has this formulation become. It is possible that Ebenezer Howard saw Riverside while he was living in Chicago in the 1870s.

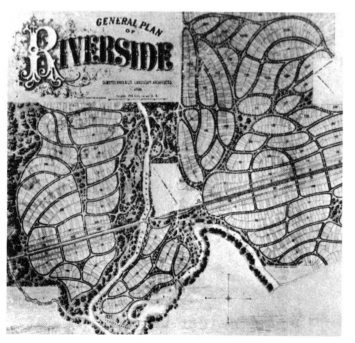

61

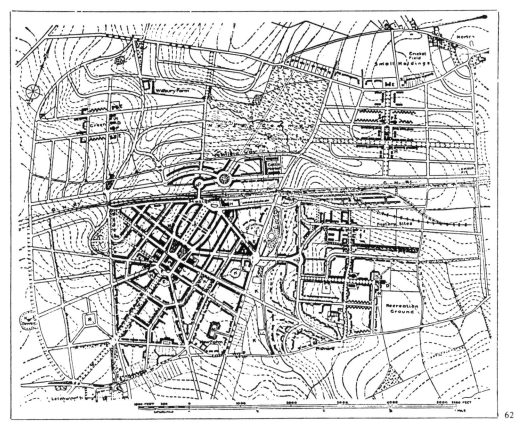

62

62, 63: Unwin and Parker's plan for Letchworth, the first garden city, and drawings showing how the designers had translated Howard's radical social ideas into an utterly unthreatening environment.

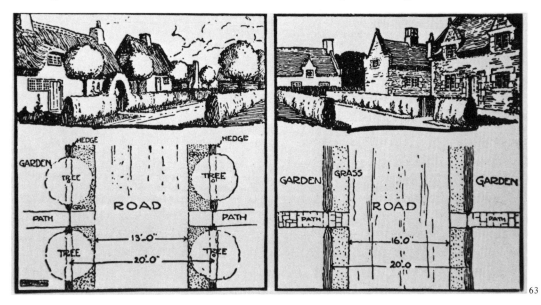

63

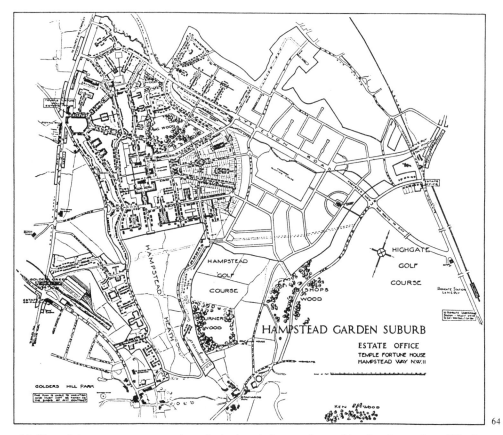

64

64: The cul-de-sac, now a commonplace of suburban design, can be considered an innovation of Unwin and Parker's. Up to this time it had usually been associated with slum housing crammed into back lots, and it would require an act of Parliament to revise the bylaws in order to use the cul-de-sac at Hampstead Garden Suburb, as shown in the plan above.

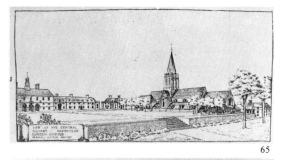

65

65, 66: Drawings of Hampstead from Raymond Unwin's 1909 book, *Town Planning in Practice.* Edwin Lutyens was associated with Unwin and Parker for the design of the center of Hampstead and was the architect for the two churches and the surrounding housing. By the time Unwin and Parker began the design of Hampstead, Unwin had read Camillo Sitte and was clearly influenced not only by Sitte's ideas about spatial enclosure but also by some of Sitte's favorite German examples. The plan of Hampstead seems more tightly organized and more architectural than that of Letchworth, benefiting from Sitte's ideas and Lutyens's architectural sophistication.

66

67

67, 68: Plan of Forest Hills Gardens, a model suburb on the Hampstead model, designed by Grosvenor Atterbury and Frederick L. Olmsted, Jr., and built in suburban New York by the Russell Sage Foundation. The architecture of Station Square at Forest Hills Gardens seems to have a somewhat Germanic appearance, like some of Unwin's sketches for Hampstead. The photograph was taken during a Fourth of July celebration and reflects the community spirit that characterized Forest Hills Gardens in its early days.

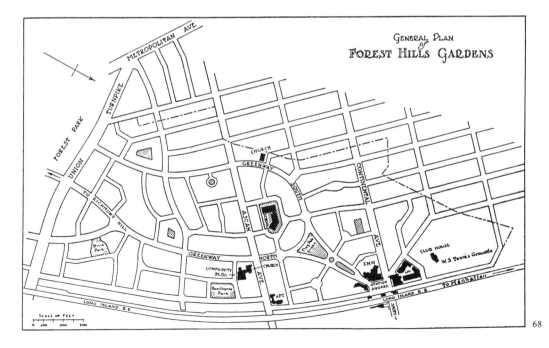

68

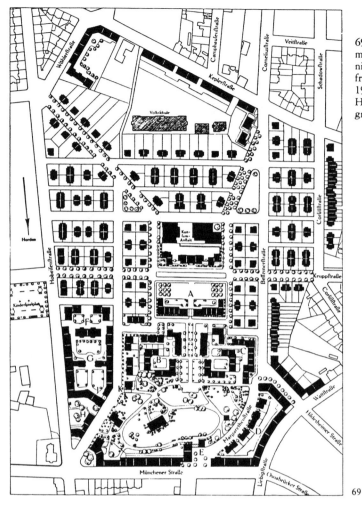

69: Plan of Alfredshof near Essen, one of the model company towns built by the Krupp munitions works. The upper part of the plan dates from the 1890s; the lower part, dating from 1910, seems to show the influence of work at Hampstead, particularly in the courtyard groups of buildings, 70.

69

70

71: Linden Court in St. Martin's, Pennsylvania, by Edmund B. Gilchrist. This group of large houses is organized in a way similar to courtyard compositions of individual houses at Hampstead.

72: The design for Tyrone, New Mexico, by Bertram G. Goodhue, translated the garden city into a Spanish vernacular. Away from the formally organized town center, rows of workmen's houses were loosely planned along winding hillside roads.

73

74: GENERAL PLAN
· ECLIPSE PARK DEVELOPMENT ·
· BELOIT · WISCONSIN ·

GEO. B. POST & SONS
ARCHITECTS & TOWN PLANNERS
101 PARK AVENUE   NEW YORK CITY

73, 74: George B. Post's design for Eclipse Park in Beloit, Wisconsin, for the employees of Fairbanks, Morse and Company, bears a distinct resemblance to Forest Hills Gardens, although the houses were more modest.

74

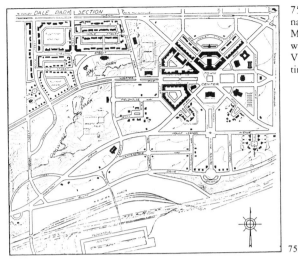

75: Mariemont, a model suburb of Cincinnati, was originally financed as a limited-profit development by Mary M. Emery and was designed by John Nolen. The plan with its central square bears a resemblance to Yorkship Village, below, which was designed at much the same time.

75

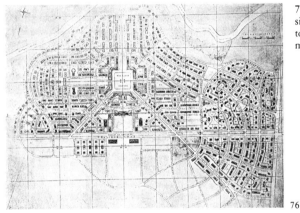

76: Yorkship Village near Camden, New Jersey, designed by Electus D. Litchfield, was one of the company towns financed by the U.S. government as part of the mobilization for World War I.

76

77: Clarence Perry's diagram of a neighborhood unit from his article published in the First Regional Plan for New York City in 1929 seems to rely strongly on the plan of Forest Hills Gardens, and on plans like the ones on this page, in abstracting a set of basic principles from contemporary practice.

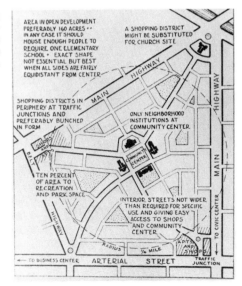

77

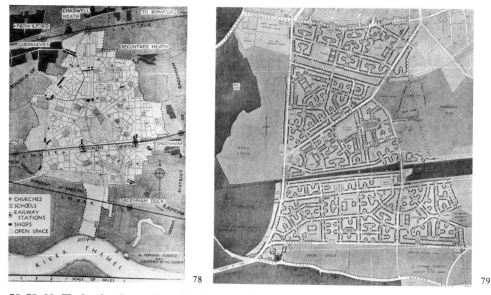

78, 79, 80: The London County Council built a series of large planned suburban communities after World War I at the density of 12 to 15 families per acre, which was advocated by Raymond Unwin in his 1912 pamphlet *Nothing Gained by Overcrowding.* All were designed under the direction of C. Topham Forrest, architect to the London County Council, or his successor, E. P. Wheeler. The largest of these London communities is Beacontree, planned in 1920 for a population of 115,000. Most of the buildings are in the English cottage vernacular, and the detailed site plan shows how much this development, and other L.C.C. work of the period, owe to Letchworth and Hampstead.

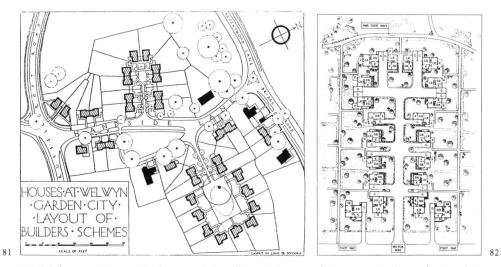

81: Cul-de-sacs at Welwyn Garden City, designed in 1921 by Louis de Soissons, the planner for the whole development. **82:** The cul-de-sac street system at Radburn, a planned community in Fairlawn, New Jersey, designed by Clarence Stein and Henry Wright as the American counterpart of the English garden city, improves on similar arrangements in British practice by making the garden side of the houses part of a complete open-space system, visible in the perspective drawing, **83.** Barry Parker then incorporated Radburn's redefined cul-de-sac into his design for Wythenshawe, a suburban housing development in Manchester, with intentions similar to those at Beacontree.

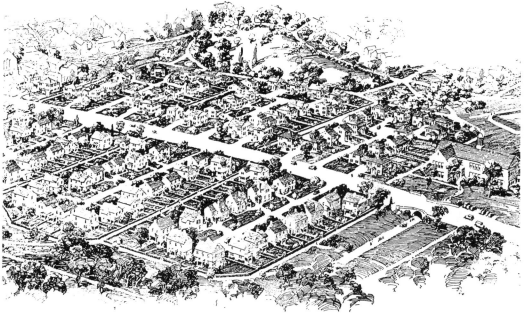

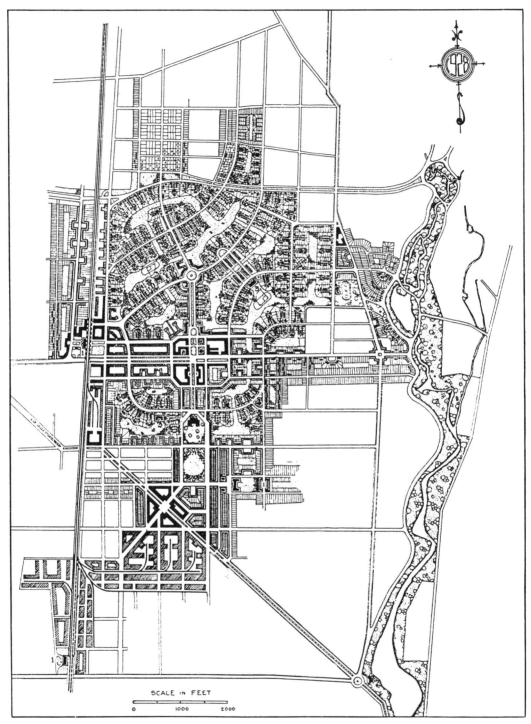

SCALE IN FEET

0   1000   2000

84

84: The Great Depression intervened after only one segment of Radburn had been constructed. The complete design was for a self-contained community on the model set forth by Ebenezer Howard.

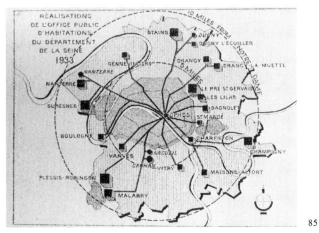

85: Satellite garden cities to be built around Paris had become government policy by the 1930s.

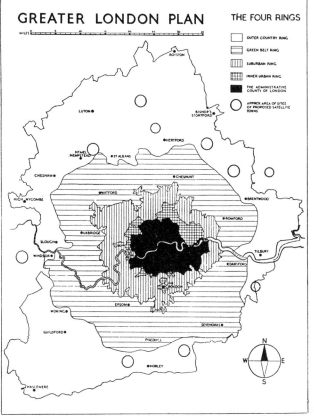

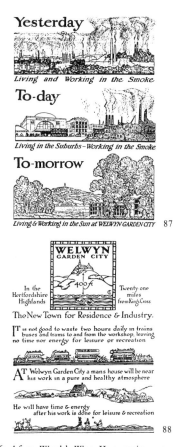

86: After World War II a major new-towns policy was inaugurated in Britain, but its primary purpose was the control of population in London and other large centers. The concept of the self-contained garden city as a means of social transformation, shown in these advertisements from the 1920s for Welwyn, 87, 88, was lost, although large numbers of new towns were being built.

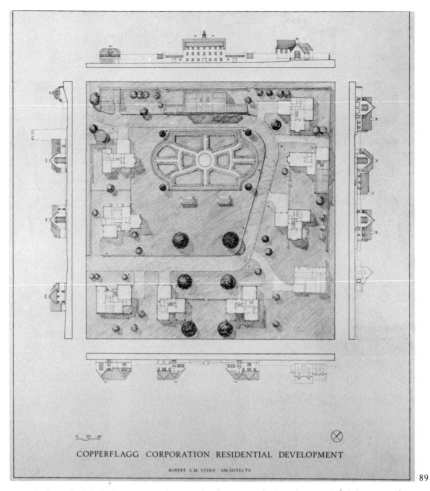

COPPERFLAGG CORPORATION RESIDENTIAL DEVELOPMENT

ROBERT A.M. STERN ARCHITECTS

89

89: Robert A. M. Stern is an architect who has now designed several subdivisions for upper-income people—such as this one on the old Flagg estate in Staten Island, New York—which are very close both architecturally and scenically to the garden suburbs of the 1920s.

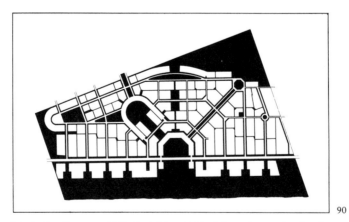

90

90: Andres Duany and Elizabeth Plater-Zyberk have designed a Florida resort community, Seaside, which has a conceptual organization not unlike Mariemont or Yorkship Village, as shown by this figure-ground plan describing lots and streets.

4
The Modern City

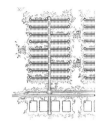

The migration of urban growth out of the central city in the direction established by the rich and fashionable, a pattern that can be seen as early as the development of Covent Garden in the 1630s, had completely reshaped cities by 1920. The movement of people with economic choice had been hastened by the industrialization of older parts of the city and the resulting pollution and slums.

The financial district remained in the heart of the older city, as did the wholesale markets, and—very often—the seat of city government. Farther out in the fashionable direction would be more recent office buildings, a cluster of department stores, and the theater and entertainment district. Next, continuing outward in the same sector of the city, would be a midtown area with a mixture of hotels, office buildings and the more expensive shops. Beyond midtown would be the nineteenth-century mansion district, parks, the art museum and, often, the most important local university, which otherwise had probably remained on an older site downtown. There might then be a break of industrial land and poverty districts before fashionable city neighborhoods, along approximately the same vector of growth, and then the new fashionable suburbs and the estates of the very rich.

Every city also had an unfashionable direction. In a small town, people might speak of the "right" and "wrong" sides of the tracks; in bigger cities there would be vast areas that were most definitely wrong: the site for railroad yards, factories and the neighborhoods of workers' housing, usually built to minimal standards and lying under a cloud of pollution from railroads and factories.

London, the first large city to grow in this way, can be considered the prototype. The West End was "right," the East End "wrong." The financial district remained in the City, the original central area. Westward were the wholesale districts that had taken over Covent Garden, the theater and entertainment district around Shaftesbury Avenue and Leicester Square, the department stores on Oxford Street, a midtown area running from Marble Arch to Knightsbridge alongside the fashionable residential districts of Mayfair and Belgravia, and then, on the south side of Hyde Park, the museums and universities of South Kensington.

Very much the same pattern could be found in any city that developed in response to the real-estate market during the nineteenth and early twentieth centuries.

In New York City, the fashionable direction ran northward along Broadway and Fifth Avenue. The financial district remained downtown on Wall Street, with City Hall just to the north up Broadway and the market districts mostly just to the northwest. Strung out along the fashionable vector were the department store district at Herald Square, the theater district at Times Square, midtown along Fifth Avenue up to Central Park, and then the expensive residential neighborhoods of the Upper East Side.

In Cleveland the fashionable vector ran eastward from the wholesale markets on the Flats and the financial district near Public Square and out Euclid Avenue past the department stores and the midtown district, through what in the 1920s was still a neighborhood of mansions, to university, park and museum, and beyond to suburbs like Shaker Heights.

In Pittsburgh the fashionable direction was also to the east, in Baltimore it ran north up Charles Street; in Atlanta, north on Peachtree; in New Orleans, west on St. Charles Avenue. In Kansas City the fashionable direction was established to the south, toward the country club district; in San Francisco development ran westward up California Street and on to Pacific Heights.

Many cities also had a sibling across a river or harbor—often with a different name and political identity—which would be a junior version of its larger and more distinguished neighbor, and would possess its own business districts, fashionable vector, museums and other institutions, as well as the inevitable factories and slums. New York and Brooklyn were one such pair; Philadelphia and Camden; Kansas City, Missouri, and Kansas City, Kansas; San Francisco and Oakland.

Some of the best portraits of the North American city around 1920 are contained in the opening chapters of Sinclair Lewis's *Babbitt,* published in 1922. Here is George Babbitt driving to his office downtown, "where the towers of Zenith aspired above the morning mist," from his home in the garden suburb of Floral Heights, on the fashionable southeast side of the city:

> He admired each district along his familiar route to the office: The bungalows and shrubs and winding irregular driveways of Floral Heights. The one-story shops on Smith Street, a glare of plate glass and new yellow brick; groceries and laundries and drug stores to supply the more immediate needs of East Side housewives. The market gardens in Dutch Hollow, their shanties patched with corrugated iron and stolen doors. Billboards with crimson goddesses nine feet tall advertising cinema films, pipe tobacco and talcum powder. The old "mansions" along Ninth Street, S.E., like aged dandies in filthy linen; wooden castles turned into boarding houses, with muddy walks and rusty hedges, jostled by fast-intruding garages, cheap apartment houses, and fruit stands . . . Across the belt of railroad-tracks, factories with high-perched water tanks and tall stacks—factories producing condensed milk, paper boxes, lighting fixtures, motor cars. Then the business center, the thickening, darting traffic, the crammed trolleys unloading, and high doorways of marble and polished granite.

This city, so different from the compact cities of low buildings and horse-drawn traffic of one hundred years before, had evolved with comparatively little theoretical discussion as to what the appropriate form of a modern city should be. Public buildings were probably grouped according to the principles of monumental design, the street leading through the mansion district might be a boulevard, and the fashionable outer residential areas were garden suburbs. Otherwise the surveyor and the investor were of a great deal more importance than the designer in determining the layout of streets and the subdivision of property. Where the preindustrial city had been contained by walls and had evolved over many centuries, the modern city grew and changed rapidly in response to the real-estate market.

The early decades of the twentieth century saw the beginning of the modern profession of city planning, and the first theoretical discussions of recent city development by Patrick Geddes, but few specialists in cities at this time wrote of the need to transform cities in every detail so that they would be appropriate to the modern world.

This relative lack of discussion about modernism in cities contrasted with the sharp controversies about the effect of modern technology on architecture that had already begun by the end of the nineteenth century.

Structural steel, large sheets of glass, the invention of the safety elevator and of artificial lighting and climate control made possible buildings that could never have been constructed before the modern period. At the same time, new building types were evolving for factories and offices, hospitals and institutions. These innovations were incorporated into architectural design as soon it was technologically and economically feasible to do so. The question that remained to be answered, however, was what effect technological change should have on architectural expression.

In 1895, the Austrian architect Otto Wagner wrote a textbook, *Modern Architecture,* in which he stated that "the whole basis of the views of architecture prevailing today must be displaced by the recognition that the only possible point of departure for our artistic creation is modern life."

A typical pronouncement from the other side was made by H. Heathcote Statham—editor of the influential English publication *The Builder*—in a book, also entitled *Modern Architecture,* that was published in 1897. Statham concluded his discussion of technology by stating that the idea that the new steel structure "is to revolutionize modern architecture I hold therefore to be a complete fallacy, based on bad reasoning and on a confusion between engineering and architecture."

Until recently Wagner's statement would have been judged to represent the attitude that was eventually to prevail and Statham's view as a laughable misjudgment. Even Statham's own book showed that the steel frame and the elevator had already revolutionized architecture by permitting buildings to be much taller than any but ornamental structures had ever been in the past. However, the question of architectural expression was not to be permanently settled. Architects who are popularly referred to as "postmodern" have moved back to something like Statham's position, with designs that are derived from preindustrial construction systems like the column, the arch and the vault, despite the advanced technology actually being used.

Nevertheless, the idea that modern architecture should be qualitatively different from the architecture of the past has had an enormous effect on the design of the modern city. Some architects who were pioneers of new architectural expression remained relatively conservative about city design, others sought to remake the city, either as a by-product of their polemical positions about architecture, or in order to achieve a complete break with the buildings of the past.

The first fully developed design intended as a specifically modern city was the Cité Industrielle of Tony Garnier. Garnier, as a young architect from Lyons, had won the prestigious Grand Prix de Rome in 1899, and then used his five years at the Villa Medici to develop a project for a complete industrial city, instead of the customary archaeological study of Roman ruins, which Garnier managed to keep to a minimum. The Cité Industrielle was first exhibited in 1901, and Garnier continued to elaborate on the designs, which were ultimately published in 1917. The concept has some affinities with Ebenezer Howard's garden city in its low densities and the use of greenbelts, and may indeed have been influenced by it; but the intention was substantially different. Garnier was interested in developing detailed architectural designs for a complete manufacturing city, and in creating a new land-use pattern that separated manufacturing, residence and recreation far more completely than at Letchworth. He did not share Howard's interest in transforming society by making existing cities obsolete.

The civic center of the Cité Industrielle was flanked on both sides by residential neighborhoods, these areas were separated from the railway yards, port and industrial districts by a park, and the whole city was surrounded by parklands. Garnier had worked out the architecture of the housing and designed the principal buildings for his city, using poured reinforced concrete, then an unusual new building material.

The arrangement of the blocks was consistent with monumental city-design principles, but the architecture, while essentially similar to Beaux Arts building forms, was stripped of all historic details. The relative austerity of the buildings depicted in Garnier's drawings was at least partly a response to the concept of a utilitarian, industrial city; it was also a statement about the nature of cities in a modern world.

Garnier was appointed city architect of Lyons in 1904, and was able to use his theoretical studies as the basis for many actual buildings. In

1920, after leaving the office of city architect, Garnier prepared designs for the États-Unis district of Lyons, which over the next fifteen years was developed as a complete residential neighborhood, using some of the housing types that had been originally thought out for the Cité Indus-trielle.

Hendrik Berlage, who had designed the Amsterdam Stock Exchange in 1896 in what was viewed at the time as a radically simplified form of architecture, first drew the plan for the Amsterdam South district in 1902, and then revised it in 1915, after a trip Berlage had made to the United States in 1911. The 1915 plan clearly shows the influence of Burnham's monumental plan for Chicago, but the architecture suggested is in the Northern European tradition of brick walls and high-pitched gabled roofs, rather than the Parisian classicism of Burnham's Haussmannesque plan.

The buildings implementing this plan, by architects of the so-called Amsterdam School, such as Michel de Klerk and Piet Kramer, as well as Berlage himself, while specifically intended to be a modern style of archi-tecture, created a low-scaled and warm environment, with idiosyncratic details that were evocative of Northern European folk architectural tradi-tions. The spatial organization was essentially the familiar street and court-yard; the unified architecture, the generosity of the open space and the planting of the gardens made the qualitative difference.

A totally different philosophy about the modern city was shown in drawings of a contemporary city for three million people displayed at the Paris Salon d'Automne in 1922 by the Swiss-French architect Charles-Édouard Jeanneret, who called himself Le Corbusier. According to Le Corbusier, the organizers had asked him to prepare an exhibit on urban-ism, by which they had meant the elements of civic design that tradition-ally lent themselves to "artistic" treatment, such as fountains, street light-ing and signs. Le Corbusier's response was to attempt the design of an entire city of three million people, the size that Paris had grown to at the time.

The drawings for this exhibition should be seen in the context of articles that Le Corbusier had been writing for the periodical *L'Ésprit Nouveau,* including those collected and published the following year as *Vers une Architecture,* familiar to readers of English in Frederick Etchells's 1927 translation, *Towards a New Architecture.* One of the points that Le

Corbusier made in this book, under the heading "Eyes Which Do Not See," was that the design of ocean liners, airplanes and automobiles had already achieved a new expression, free of remembered elements from the past. It was time to do the same for architecture. Le Corbusier's Ville Contemporaine would demonstrate what a modern city could look like if it were created solely out of buildings appropriate to the modern age.

The city was designed on a rectangular grid, in proportion rather like the blocks of midtown Manhattan. At the center of this projected city was a transportation terminal for automobiles, trains and underground transit located at the intersection of two broad highways, one running precisely north-south, the other east-west. On the roof of the terminal was a landing field, which made the center complete but created a hazardous approach path for the biplanes that flit like moths through Le Corbusier's renderings, as there was to be a sixty-story, cross-shaped office building at each of the four corners of the terminal roof, which was flanked by four additional identical towers, two on the east and two on the west.

Sixteen more office towers, all a uniform sixty stories high, surrounded the city center, forming a larger rectangle along the east-west axis. All the towers were separated by parkland, which, within the rigid geometry of the city's rectangular street network, had the informal qualities of the English garden. The inner office rectangle around the terminal was surrounded by a multilevel shopping center of promenades and terraces. The most famous drawing of the series portraying this city shows a terrace restaurant in the shopping center looking toward the transportation terminal across the intervening parkland.

The elite of the city were to live within a diamond-shaped area around the central core, the diamond created by a second road network, at forty-five-degree angles to the first, that formed a system of diagonal boulevards. The buildings within the diamond were to be luxurious apartment hotels, with communal maid service and restaurants. Also within the diamond were municipal offices and other public buildings. The remainder of the blocks in the central area were also residential. At the western end of the city was an enormous park, designed as an English garden, occupying the position that the Bois de Boulogne takes in the plan of Paris but in shape much more like Central Park in Manhattan.

The entire central section of the city with its business skyscrapers and apartment houses was surrounded by an enormous greenbelt. Beyond the greenbelt were satellite cities for industry and workers' housing. Two thirds of the city's population were to live in these satellites.

The concept thus depends very heavily upon earlier design ideas for cities: the long, straight streets and diagonal avenues of the monumental tradition; the idea, also from the monumental tradition, that city buildings should be of uniform height and architecture; plus Garnier's concept of a specifically industrial city, which became separate communities, something like Howard's model, beyond a Howardesque greenbelt. At the same time, Le Corbusier is the first to give definitive artistic expression to the importance of the automobile and the tall building in the design of cities. He understood that the logic of the elevator building suggests a freestanding structure, not a subunit in a street of similar facades; that the automobile was likely to become the dominant mode of urban transportation, lending itself to uniform street-grid patterns, but with streets spaced farther apart than traditional urban blocks; and that the need for unimpeded automobile movement would create the limited-access highways that appear in his renderings long before anyone actually built one.

Le Corbusier went on to apply these ideas to central Paris in the Voisin Plan, exhibited in 1925. In this proposal, eighteen sixty-floor skyscrapers and three clusters of luxury apartments borrowed from the earlier design of the contemporary city replace the business center of Paris, and a limited-access highway is driven straight through the heart of the city. Notre Dame and the Louvre survive, but the traditional fabric of central Paris is obliterated.

Paris in the 1920s, like London or New York, had a financial district centered on the stock exchange, a downtown market district (Les Halles), and a nearby center of city government. The fashionable direction led westward past the theaters, past the department stores on the Boulevard Haussmann, to the midtown district that extended up the Champs Élysées, and beyond to the exclusive residences of the Seventeenth Arrondissement. The fashionable suburbs were generally to the west; the unfashionable side of the city was to the east. Le Corbusier's proposal had a uniform, repetitive building pattern; it made no acknowledgment of the different functional districts and diverse neighborhood character to be found in central Paris.

There were certainly good reasons to be dissatisfied with cities in the 1920s. Rapid growth and unregulated industrialization during the nineteenth century created terrible living conditions for the poor in slum districts that occupied large urban areas. By the beginning of the twentieth century, some of the worst sanitation and water-supply problems had been overcome, and laws now regulated what developers could build, but these laws were hardly stringent and often unenforced. The average worker's dwelling was dark and crowded and had only rudimentary plumbing. But Le Corbusier sought to obliterate not the working-class districts of Paris but the area with the highest real-estate values. While Le Corbusier's priorities were to change later, his original vision of a new order was designed for the elite.

Le Corbusier was a great artist who was able to capture the promise and excitement of modernity in extraordinarily authoritative images, but the images were not based on the functional organization or economic priorities of real cities.

The Voisin Plan also embodies a belief in the centralization of power and responsibility that was to find expression in the urban-renewal projects and city rebuilding that took place after the Second World War. There was a contempt for the existing city and faith in the superior wisdom of the city designer. Le Corbusier himself made no secret of his belief that city design required an autocratic government that would put someone like himself in charge of all new building. He even made a little sketch of the government decree that he believed should put the implementation of the Voisin Plan in motion. For Le Corbusier, power was more important than ideology. He was a member of the proto-fascist Redressement Français during the 1920s, sought to work for the Soviets, visited Italy and wrote favorably of Mussolini, and then spent eighteen months after the German occupation in 1941 trying to persuade the Nazi-sponsored Vichy government of France to implement his plan for Algiers.

In the 1920s, urban construction and reconstruction were not yet taking place on the scale imagined by Le Corbusier; and to his intense disappointment, his drawings had little immediate influence. What was happening throughout Europe during the period between the two world wars was the creation of many new working-class residential districts, subsidized by governments and designed to new, higher standards.

From the end of the First World War until Catherine Bauer's tabulation for her influential book *Modern Housing,* which was published in

1934, more than 4.5 million dwelling units were built in Western Europe with some kind of governmental subsidy, some 70 percent of all housing constructed. An average of approximately 15 percent of the population lived in state-aided dwellings by the end of the period.

Some of this new development took place at low densities on the garden-city pattern, particularly in England; but in many European cities the organization of these neighborhoods had a more urban character. These developments either followed street frontages and formed courts and hollow squares inside the blocks, as in the new southern districts of Amsterdam, or they were arranged in open-ended rows, often at right angles to streets, with buildings placed for the best possible orientation, a method of design given a definitive form by the German architect Otto Haesler, in a series of row-housing developments from 1923 onward.

Many architects of these new housing projects, particularly in Germany and the Netherlands, were, like Haesler, believers in a new, "objective" form of architecture, stripped of romantic forms and historical associations. During the 1920s, however, there was not always a predictable correlation between the choice of courtyard or row, and the employment of objectivity or historical reminiscence. Some courtyard groups were composed of austere buildings with stripped surfaces and flat roofs, while some housing planned in parallel rows had pitched roofs and dormer windows.

The Weissenhof Housing Settlement, planned by the Deutscher Werkbund for the city of Stuttgart in 1927, was intended to be both a residential district and an exhibition of the potentialities of a more austere form of modern architecture. Ludwig Mies van der Rohe, the first vice-president of the Werkbund, was the master planner and organizer. Mies was then forty-one years old and just beginning the career that was to make him one of the most influential modern architects.

In the central, prominent place on the site plan was an apartment house by Mies himself. The design of two prefabricated houses was contributed by Walter Gropius, the head of the Bauhaus trade school and workshops in Dessau, an institution that was to become almost synonymous with modern design. A second, smaller apartment building was designed by Peter Behrens, for whom Mies, Le Corbusier and Walter Gropius had worked when they were just starting out. There were row houses by the Dutch architects J. J. P. Oud and Mart Stam, and individual houses or pairs of houses by other important architects who were seeking new solutions to problems of architectural expression or style: Le Corbusier in partnership with his cousin Pierre Jeanneret, Max Taut, Bruno Taut, Hans Poelzig and Hans Scharoun. In the farthest corner of the site was a house by Victor Bourgeois, whose Cité Moderne at Berchem-Sainte-Agathe near Brussels, begun in 1922, could be considered the prototype housing development designed in an intentionally modern style.

Among those conspicuously not included in the Weissenhof demonstration were Ernst May, the city architect of Frankfurt, who had already begun work on the Praunheim and Romerstadt districts described in the previous chapter, and Otto Haesler.

Perhaps because of the force of Mies's personality, perhaps because of conscious cooperation, or perhaps through historical coincidence, the Weissenhof buildings showed a remarkable stylistic unity. All the buildings had flat roofs; they all emphasized the use of industrial materials, like steel and concrete, and had plain wall surfaces finished in white. Mies and Le Corbusier used their buildings to show the flexibility of the floor plans made possible when structure and enclosure could be separated by means of the steel frame.

While not impressive as a piece of city planning, Weissenhof thus seemed important as a statement about architectural style. The chaos and confusion of the nineteenth-century city, the stylistic shifts from classic to gothic to other styles of architecture, the difficulty of assimilating the new scale of development permitted by the elevator and the steel frame, all made the display of unity at Weissenhof appear to be the potential forerunner of a new universal architecture.

In the Europe of the late 1920s a consensus did seem to be emerging as a modern formula for housing development. It accepted Haesler's design determinants: orientation for maximum sunlight, buildings at right angles to traffic streets, and buildings spaced in relation to height so that they would not block sun from each other. The Dammerstock district of Karlsruhe, planned by Walter Gropius in 1929, with buildings by Gropius and other architects, is representative. The Rothenberg housing development at Kassel, planned and designed by Otto Haesler just before Hitler took over the German government, was the example of recent German housing given the most attention in the 1932 modern architecture exhibition at the Museum of Modern Art. Except for one curving row of houses along a principal street, it is composed entirely of parallel rows without any spatial enclosure.

"Modern Architecture," the exhibition prepared by Henry-Russell Hitchcock and Philip Johnson and presented at the then newly formed Museum of Modern Art in 1932, was accompanied by their book, *The International Style.* Alfred Barr, the museum's director, stated in an introduction that the authors

> have proven beyond any reasonable doubt . . . that there exists today a modern style as original, as consistent, as logical and as widely distributed as any in the past.

Johnson and Hitchcock themselves made the following statement in the opening chapter of *The International Style:*

> The idea of style, which began to degenerate when the revivals destroyed the disciplines of the Baroque, has become real and fertile again. Today a single new style has come into existence.

The intellectual justification for this statement could only have been that it was a prediction, as the buildings at Weissenhof or the workers' housing districts produced by a few modernist architects during the closing days of the Weimar Republic were unlike the work of most architects of the time: indeed, that was the whole point. From our vantage point today we know that whatever the descriptive merits of "International Style" as a term, the predictions of singularity or universality were never to be fulfilled. Even to make the prediction in 1932 the exhibition had to leave out much of the work of important modernist architects like Hans Scharoun and Erich Mendelsohn, and omitted Hugo Haring altogether. Frank Lloyd Wright was given a prominent position in the exhibition, but was treated as a spiritual ancestor of the new international modernism, rather than as a practitioner actively pursuing a different type of design.

By 1932 the work of the architects exhibited was already beginning to diverge from the apparent similarities that formed the basis for the International Style as a hypothesis. Le Corbusier was starting down the road that was to lead him to Ronchamp; J. J. P. Oud was to be the author of buildings that we would now call Art Deco; Mies was to be increasingly influenced by the organizing principles of monumental architecture, culminating in the almost neoclassical plan of the Seagram Building (designed, ironically, in collaboration with Philip Johnson). By the 1950s even the firm headed by Walter Gropius, who had done so much to foster the development of European modernism, was using neo-Islamic ornament and architectural form in proposals for the University of Baghdad.

But in the mid-1930s, the concept of a universal modern architectural style still seemed a tenable hypothesis; and the modernist theory of site planning began to impose a new kind of uniformity on city design, with orientation and sunlight, rather than streets and courtyards, determining architectural form. In the revised plan for the southern districts of Amsterdam in 1934, the year of Berlage's death, Berlage's monumental street plan was replaced by housing at right angles to streets arranged in parallel rows for orientation, with each building separated by approximately its own height from the next parallel structure. This plan is shown approvingly in Sigfried Giedion's *Space, Time and Architecture* as the admirable triumph of modernism over Berlage's well-intentioned but only half-modern ideas.

The revised Amsterdam plan reflected concepts shown at the third meeting of the Congrès Internationaux d'Architecture Moderne, held at Brussels in 1930. C.I.A.M., founded in 1928, brought together leading modernist architects of Europe, including Gropius, Mies and Le Corbusier, to compare work and to compose manifestos and statements of architectural philosophy. Cor van Eesteren, then newly appointed as head of the Amsterdam Town Planning Department, was elected president of C.I.A.M. at the Brussels meeting, which marked a change of direction for C.I.A.M., toward a concern with modern city design.

The fourth C.I.A.M. meeting, of which Le Corbusier was an influential organizer, took place on board the S.S. *Patris II,* sailing from Marseilles to Athens and back again in 1933, and adopted a series of statements of principle about city planning. The four critical areas of city planning were seen to be dwellings, recreation, workplaces and transportation. Most people were expected to live in apartments, and tall buildings were to be used whenever there were high densities in order to free the ground for recreation and permit exposure to sunlight. Housing was to be grouped according to the neighborhood theory that had originated with Clarence Perry, with the size of the neighborhood determined by relationships to the school system. Work places were to be located where they minimized transportation requirements and did not adversely affect neighboring areas. Transportation principles included the classification of streets according to function and the provision of highways for high-speed traffic, and traditional monumental city planning was faulted for creating traffic problems.

There is a statement in favor of preserving "buildings or groups of buildings that are remnants of past cultures," but these past cultures are assumed to be irrelevant to the modern world and it is made clear that major changes in cities are necessary. Zoning was seen to be the most important means of carrying out planning objectives both in older parts of cities and in new developments. But there is no discussion of the functional zones already present in cities or of the social distinctions that established the character of most existing residential neighborhoods.

While the tall building was officially adopted by C.I.A.M. as a basic design element of cities, actual European housing projects were almost always row houses or walk-up apartments; elevators were used sparingly in European low-income housing before the Second World War. La Cité de La Muette at Drancy, near Paris, designed by Beaudoin and Lods and built in the late 1930s, was one of the few exceptions. It had fifteen-story apartment towers placed at the ends of parallel rows of conventional three- and four-story buildings.

There was almost no European experience with the creation of tall buildings in existing cities during the interwar period, and those that were constructed were generally designed to minimize the appearance of height. Only occasionally is a tall building used in a situation where its height is emphasized. One example is the Victorieplein apartment tower by J. F. Staal, which acts as a major accent within Berlage's Amsterdam South plan.

The careful positioning of this tower as the focal point of intersecting avenues, in a setting of uniformly low buildings, is unlike the concept of city design implied by the photomontages showing projects for tall, glass-curtain-wall buildings designed by Ludwig Mies van der Rohe during the 1920s. Mies simply interpolates his structures into the old context on sites that had the potential for new development. Meant to create an impression of a desirable architecture, these montages seem today to be prophetic of the discontinuity of scale and disruption of the urban fabric created by this building type in the years since the Second World War. C.I.A.M. meetings were not, however, troubled by any misgivings about tall buildings in existing cities.

Le Corbusier's ideas about cities had continued to evolve as a result of his own experience and his association with C.I.A.M. In 1929 he had made a trip to South America and sketched plans for transforming Rio de Janeiro, São Paulo, Montevideo and Buenos Aires. In several of these plans he had drawn gigantic new highways that cut across the terrain like Roman aqueducts, with the spaces under the highways filled with apartments. A highway that was also a dwelling place for 180,000 people was a feature of Le Corbusier's 1930 plan for Algiers, which included a complete transformation of the waterfront district into a group of gigantic office buildings, linked by a bridge to a new group of massive apartment buildings on the heights above the city. Le Corbusier wrote that the effect of this plan on Algiers would be like artillery shells—indicating that the idea was intended to destroy existing concepts of the city as much as it was intended as a serious design. The Algiers plans were to continue to have an important influence, helping architects to create concepts of cities as buildings when that idea became important in the 1960s.

In 1935 Le Corbusier prepared a revision of his theoretical city construct, now called La Ville Radieuse. Its social structure reflected his flirtation at the time with the authoritarian organization advocated by the syndicalists; its plan had a new anthropomorphic appearance, with an administrative head (the familiar cluster of cross-shaped office towers), a residential body with commercial-district viscera, workers' housing for legs and factories for feet. The influence of the recently adopted C.I.A.M. principles may perhaps be seen in the increasing articulation of separate districts, but the nature and placement of these districts did not correspond to the functional organization of existing cities.

Le Corbusier's second sketch plan for Buenos Aires, 1938, has an administrative district of five tall buildings constructed as an island in the harbor and linked to the mainland by a causeway; the waterfront is rebuilt as a recreation center; and a new transportation system of limited-access highways and major roads carves the body of the city into sectors. Within the sectors, tall buildings and open areas were to replace the existing texture of the city.

The plan was not a polemic but a seriously intended program for what were to become significant public policies almost everywhere in the years after the Second World War. All the essential features of postwar urban renewal are present: the highways that cut through existing buildings and neighborhoods, the total reconstruction of business and residential districts, clusters of tall towers, and buildings designed to bridge over highways.

Le Corbusier's 1938 plan for Algiers was also meant as a program for practical change. Its most prominent features were the reconstruction of the business center as a single enormous office tower, the replacement of the former business district with a recreational and civic center, and the creation of a new suburban residential area composed of towers.

A common factor in all of these plans is Le Corbusier's ability to contemplate city design with almost total disregard for the accumulated buildings and organizational relationships of the existing metropolis. Other C.I.A.M. members also seemed to think of city design as replacing, not modifying, the existing metropolis. The devastation of war was to add to the belief that out of destruction could come an opportunity for cities to make a new start.

The MARS (Modern Architectural Research) group, the English component of C.I.A.M., drew up a plan for the London metropolitan region in the early 1940s that drove a great expressway through the city just to the north of the historic central area. Business districts were to extend in an east-west corridor on either side of the historic center. Linear residential districts, each housing up to 600,000 people and separated from each other by greenbelts, would be placed at right angles to the central development corridor and connected by a circular highway running around the outside of the metropolis. The diagram for this concept looks like a vastly inflated version of the cul-de-sacs in a garden-city neighborhood. A similar impulse to take garden-city design principles up to a gigantic scale can be seen in Ludwig Hilberseimer's 1944 Ruralization of the Metropolis plan, where corridors of parkland separate relatively dense neighborhoods in which housing has been laid out in straight rows.

Ideas about redesigning cities through clearance of enormous areas were to have an important impact on North America after the Second World War, but they did not evolve there. There was little communication in the interwar period between C.I.A.M. and American housing reformers and city designers.

Housing for workers in the United States during the 1920s was undertaken not by government but by charitable foundations and limited-profit housing corporations like City Investing Company, the backer of Sunnyside and Radburn. Government subsidies were introduced into housing by the 1926 New York Housing Law, which established a twenty-year tax abatement for limited-dividend projects that held rents to $11 a room ($12.50 in Manhattan).

A hollow square, with buildings around the perimeter of a block forming courtyards within, was the urban building type most used for charity-supported housing like the Dunbar apartments in New York City, and later for the New York State–subsidized Amalgamated Dwellings. The design of these buildings was closely related to subsidized housing being built in London during the 1920s and 1930s. Andrew J. Thomas was the architect who did much to define this building type in the United States, where it was characterized by brick buildings in a pleasant, vaguely historical style, surrounding handsomely landscaped gardens. His earlier buildings, such as Phipps and the Dunbar, and the Marshall Field garden apartments in Chicago, were walk-ups. Springsteen and Goldhammer's 1930 design for the six-story Amalgamated Dwellings in New York City was one of the first projects to use elevators for a hollow-square plan.

Clarence Stein, who had done so much to get garden-city planning ideas accepted in the United States, was also responsible for pioneering work in housing at higher densities. His 1930 Phipps Garden Apartments development in Sunnyside followed a hollow-square walk-up plan that was an adaptation of earlier work by Thomas. Stein's Hillside Homes near the Boston Post Road in the New York borough of the Bronx is a series of interlocking courtyards surrounded by five-story walk-up apartment houses. Some of the buildings, taking advantage of the sloping site, have an additional lower level of garden apartments directly accessible from outside.

None of these buildings sought to make any programmatic points about modernism or modern architecture. Modern construction methods were used, and the amount of open space provided was far greater than in traditional urban courtyards, but the design did not display the identifying characteristics associated with the International Style, which had largely been derived from the architectural concepts shared by the buildings in the Weissenhof exhibition. Instead of an architecture expressive of volume, studied asymmetry and the avoidance of applied decoration, the organization of buildings by Stein or Thomas was based on external mass; masses were often symmetrical, and applied decoration was used, although generally in a simplified form.

Hugh Ferris made use of a similar architectural aesthetic of mass, symmetry and simplified ornament in the drawings he prepared for his book *The Metropolis of Tomorrow,* published in 1929. Ferris, an architect and a famous architectural renderer, did not have a concept for a new social order, nor was he concerned to create a polemic for a revolutionary form of architecture. He was extrapolating from the architecture of New York City and its zoning controls during the confident 1920s. Ferris's vision is in its way as abstract and unrelated to the daily life of existing cities as Le Corbusier's Ville Contemporaine, but it is much more closely related to the real-estate and building practice of the time. The architecture is derived from designs of Ferris's American contemporaries, particularly Bertram Goodhue and Raymond Hood, and shows little European influence, apart, perhaps, from the use in some of Ferris's drawings of horizontal bands of windows and floor slabs cantilevered beyond simple, strong masses, which are similar to Johannes Duiker and Bernard Bijvoet's entry in the 1922 Chicago Tribune competition.

The center of Ferris's city was a park in which an intersecting road system inscribed a six-pointed star inset in a circle. At each of three key locations around the park was a massive cluster of buildings—one for business, one for art and one for science. Three broad streets swept through these central building clusters and became the main arterials of the districts, which led to the center. A lower level of these streets was a limited-access express highway. Other major roads occurred every twelve blocks.

Ferris used zoning regulations to resolve the paradox between the tall buildings, made possible by modern technology, and the traditional relationships between building and street that are the basis for grid and boulevard plans in the monumental tradition of city design. Buildings would be limited to six stories except at the intersection of major avenues, where clusters of tall buildings up to one hundred stories would be permitted.

The economic depression of 1929 put an end to thoughts of cities with dozens of building clusters one hundred stories high. The concept of office-tower clusters does turn up again in *The World of 1960,* the model created by Norman Bel Geddes for the General Motors Pavilion at the New York World's Fair of 1939. Bel Geddes's model is not so much design as prophecy, an accurate description of the sprawling city that was to be created by the automobile. Only the clusters of towers failed to be constructed as predicted. The real-estate market is conservative, preferring to build new office towers adjacent to previously successful buildings, rather than to pioneer a new area twelve blocks away. Ferris assumed that zoning could have overcome this tendency, but development pressures have usually proved too strong for the kind of zoning patterns implied in the visions of Ferris or Bel Geddes.

Rockefeller Center, designed by a consortium of three architectural firms in the early 1930s, comes closest to realizing the concept of the city portrayed by Ferris. The architects—Reinhard & Hofmeister; Corbett, Harrison and MacMurray; and Hood and Fouilhoux—were all people whom Ferris knew, and Ferris did the perspective studies while the design was in progress.

Rockefeller Center, as noted earlier, combines monumental axial symmetry and the modern office tower with the same device that Hugh Ferris used in his city design: six-story pavilions fronting on Fifth Avenue frame the axes of the Associated Press and RCA buildings. Elsewhere in Rockefeller Center, buildings simply rise to their full height directly from the street, producing a far less coherent set of relationships.

Rockefeller Center and the Phipps Garden Apartments and Hillside Homes can be seen as fragments of a similar vision of the city. It is unquestionably modern but is not based on a revolutionary ideology, does not seek a completely new architectural expression, and can fit incrementally into the existing urban framework.

Concepts of modern city design that fit more or less comfortably into the existing city were gradually overwhelmed in the United States by the influence of European modern architecture, which made itself felt first in the subsidized or limited-profit housing type which developed in the United States during the late 1930s, a hybrid of unrelated American and European design ideas. The brick apartment building with ingenious floor plans that had been designed by Andrew Thomas, Clarence Stein and other architects was separated from its courtyard context and turned into a freestanding tower, somewhat like a smaller version of the cross-shaped office buildings of Le Corbusier's Ville Radieuse. These towers were then placed on the site in accordance with modernist ideas about optimal orientation. Le Corbusier's hypothetical towers had been closely related to a street grid. These new towers, which were soon to become synonymous with housing projects in large cities almost everywhere in the United States, were oriented for maximum sunlight and air, like German housing during the Weimar Republic. But the German developments were designed as parallel rows of low buildings. When the same orientation principle was applied to individual apartment houses, the result was a development like the Williamsburg Houses in New York City, a slum-clearance project of the Public Works Administration designed in 1935 by an architectural team headed by Richmond Shreve and including William Lescaze and Arthur Holden. Rotated off the street grid, the buildings seemed to float free of their context in a sea of undesigned open space. This detachment from the surrounding city was to become more marked when taller buildings were constructed within similar site plans after World War II.

It was, of course, the Second World War that gave European countries an immediate need for reconstruction on an unprecedented scale. Architects and planners seem to have reached a consensus that reconstruction should be an opportunity to create a new kind of modern city, with far more open space at ground level, with highways through city centers, and with tall buildings for both offices and housing.

Faith in this modern image of the city was strong despite the existence of few built examples. The overcrowding and traffic congestion of prewar cities needed improvement, the existence of modern technology made tall buildings possible, while reconstructing older buildings with the handcrafts of a previous era seemed both too expensive and too time-consuming. But the modern city concept was also ideologically attractive, a response to the powerful images created by Le Corbusier, Mies and other modernist architects, to the writings of the advocates of modern architecture, and to the version of modernism created in Sweden.

During the Second World War, Sweden was one of the few places where building construction continued, and after the war, when reconstruction was barely beginning in many European countries, the Swedes were creating a new business center for Stockholm and new planned suburbs, which became widely emulated models.

Sven Markelius, the chief planner for Stockholm from 1944 to 1954, was perhaps the most influential architect in creating Swedish concepts of modern city design. It was under Markelius's direction that the plan for the downtown Hötorget district was prepared in the 1940s. The Sergelga-tan, the principal street in the area, became a pedestrian precinct running through a two-level shopping concourse. Above the concourse on one side was a series of five parallel office towers. Pedestrian bridges linked the roof terraces above the shopping. This combination of a shopping precinct, pedestrian bridges and an orderly arrangement of office towers was to become a familiar image.

A planned residential community and the town center for a cluster of other planned communities in suburban Stockholm, Vällingby, like the design for the Hötorget, goes back to the Stockholm Planning Office in the 1940s. Vällingby was originally thought of as the heart of a self-sufficient garden city on the Howard model, but like later Stockholm satellite towns, it has developed essentially as a high-density garden sub-urb. It brings together the winding roads and picturesque building groups of garden-city planning and the housing blocks derived from European experience in the interwar period. The courtyard groups of housing at Vällingby appear in plan to be similar to those at Hampstead Garden Suburb, but the scale is different: the constituent buildings are four stories high instead of two. There are also clusters of apartment towers averaging around twelve stories, treated informally as if they were clusters of smaller buildings. Vällingby's shopping and office district centers on a casually organized pedestrian precinct with circular fountains and playful light fixtures designed to recall trees. The architecture is equally informal, with different surface materials and variations of height programmed to create the appearance of a village-like group of buildings that grew up over time. The architecture is modern in the sense that there is no applied ornament, and the design is derived from the expression of modern structural materials. It is not heroic or futuristic: "sensible" is the adjective that most readily comes to mind.

How Le Corbusier might have treated a similar commission can be inferred from his 1945 proposal for the rebuilding of Saint-Dié. A high-way runs straight through the center of the city, forming a spine that connects all its elements. Large apartment blocks are set at right angles to the central highway and are surrounded by informal gardens. The center of the city is a rectangular raised plaza with a single tall office tower, a museum, an auditorium and other civic buildings, each a separate structure surrounded by open space, but carefully composed in a grouping that resembles abstract sculpture.

Le Corbusier, polemicist for the modern city, had only limited success in obtaining a significant role in actual postwar reconstruction. His major reconstruction commission was an apartment house in Marseilles which Le Corbusier called an Unité d'Habitation, by which he meant that the structure would be virtually a small city in itself. There was an internal shopping "street" about halfway up the building and a theater, gymnasium and nursery school with playground on the roof. The whole structure was raised several stories off the ground on massive supports, a Corbusian concept that permitted external space to flow continuously through the building but also isolated it from its surroundings.

The Unité was designed as a prototype, but proved too expensive and idiosyncratic to become government policy, although, over time, the building had a great effect on other architects. Le Corbusier modified the half-dozen later buildings he designed on a similar pattern, omitting the shops. If the shops had been more conventionally located on the ground floor, they might have drawn customers from the neighborhood; but a single building was not a sufficiently large trading area to support them.

Decisions about reconstruction in Great Britain had begun while the bombs were still falling; they included the comprehensive County of London Plan of 1943 by Patrick Abercrombie and J. H. Forshaw, and the Greater London Plan of 1944 by Abercrombie. The County of London Plan included concepts for rationalizing the railway system, a new series of concentric ring roads, and the recognition of London's traditional community structure, with a public open space and road plan being used to define and separate subdistricts of the city. As mentioned previously, the Greater London Plan included a proposal for a greenbelt around the county of London and the construction of a series of planned satellite communities beyond the greenbelt, a concept owing much to the model established by Ebenezer Howard. Both plans included detailed designs for specific areas that, as in Swedish planning of the same period, combined the city-design ideas of interwar European housing precincts with the more informal layouts associated with garden-city plans.

The rebuilding of central Coventry, the reconstruction of the East End of London, and the central shopping and office districts of the first English new towns all helped define the image of the modern city that emerged in the postwar period. Like the Swedish examples, they were sensible rather than monumental or charming. In the 1950s, after the Unité d'Habitation in Marseilles had been completed, it had a major effect on British housing design, notably in work of the architect's department of the London County Council, and the character of housing and planned communities in Great Britain changed. They became more geometrically abstract and tougher in design, with much exposed reinforced concrete in the Corbusian pattern.

The reconstruction of Rotterdam yielded another significant urban image: the Lijnbaan shopping precinct and the buildings associated with it. Designed by J. H. van den Broek and Jacob Bakema, the buildings are more geometrically controlled and more closely associated with the concepts promoted by C.I.A.M. than the Sergelgatan is; but there are strong analogies in the scale and character of the pedestrian precinct, and the way nearby tall buildings are set back at right angles to it.

In much of the postwar European reconstruction an image of a potential modern city coexists uneasily with the remaining old buildings. Gaps in street frontages are filled in with structures that have plain facades, large windows and, often, a studied asymmetry, but the older street patterns and building masses are retained. In newer districts, particularly in the socialist countries of Eastern Europe, the ideas advocated by C.I.A.M. degenerated into a stereotyped formula for city design. There were two types of housing: four- or five-story walk-ups or eleven-to-thirteen-story elevator buildings. The buildings were usually placed at right angles to streets and separated from each other by a distance approximately equal to their height. The number of apartments in a housing complex would house sufficient families to support an elementary school, an idea borrowed from Clarence Perry and the American garden-city movement. While the ingredients of the formula are all worthwhile, limiting city design in this way creates environments of unrelieved dullness.

The United States also emerged from the Second World War with a widespread belief that cities should be modernized. By the 1950s new highways were being planned to link urban centers, publicly subsidized housing was greatly expanded, the concept of commercial urban renewal had become established as the means by which government promoted development in the business center of cities, and zoning laws were restudied to encourage a more modern building type.

Sometimes new highways were driven through the center of the city, as in Boston or Seattle; in other places, like Kansas City and Cincinnati, highways were planned to encircle the downtown business center.

The image of the subsidized housing project as a series of towers sited for most beneficial orientation in a sea of undefined open space, established before the Second World War, continued to be repeated, but at ever-increasing densities, which rendered the environment increasingly inhumane.

Although the United States had been spared bomb damage, the urban-renewal policies instituted in many American cities during the 1950s produced something very like the same result. Extensive clearance was partly related to the introduction of urban highway links, but was also directed toward eliminating slums and redesigning business centers to create larger amounts of open space at ground level, with densities made up by towers.

The comprehensive revision of the New York City zoning law which was completed in 1961 was to become a prototype for many large-city zoning codes. As in urban renewal and subsidized housing, the design concept behind the ordinance was the tower surrounded by open space. Freestanding towers were encouraged by a 20 percent floor area bonus for a public open space at ground level. The architectural image behind the regulations for office buildings was almost certainly derived from the Seagram Building by Mies van der Rohe and Philip Johnson, completed in 1958, and the Chase Manhattan Bank tower by Skidmore Owings and Merrill, completed in 1960. In both cases the tower was a simple rectangular mass set free of the surrounding street system by large amounts of open space. The architectural image for residential building regulations came from tower-in-open-space projects like Parkchester, developed by the Metropolitan Life Insurance Company between 1938 and 1942, and Stuyvesant Town, a slum-clearance project that was part of a program run by Robert Moses, and was also developed by the Metropolitan Life Insurance Company, beginning in 1947. The architects for Parkchester were a board of design chaired by Richmond Shreve and including Andrew J. Eken, George Gove, Gilmore Clarke, Robert Dowling, Irwin Clavan and Henry C. Meyers, Jr. Irwin Clavan and Gilmore Clarke were the designers of Stuyvesant Town. Towers in parks on the Parkchester and Stuyvesant Town model were built into the open-space ratios and building-spacing requirements of the 1961 zoning.

As zoning regulations were rerevised to base building design on a relationship to open space rather than to streets, an incremental version of the tower-in-park city was created in many places. Towers in parks, like Le Corbusier's sixty-story office buildings in the Ville Contemporaine or the Unité d'Habitation, were not design concepts that lent themselves to incremental development. The result was often to open up views of undesigned party walls, and to create buildings that were not related to one another, amid discontinuous pockets of open space.

The urban-renewal project, where government powers of condemnation and land subsidy permitted the redevelopment of larger areas, opened up the possibility of more comprehensive modernization of city centers. Designs for many urban-renewal projects were influenced by two unexecuted concepts. One was an early plan for the redevelopment of railway yards in Boston's Back Bay, made in 1953 by a team of architects, headed by Walter Gropius, that included Pietro Belluschi, Carl Koch, Hugh Stubbins, and Walter Bogner. The other influential concept was Victor Gruen's 1956 plan for Fort Worth.

The Back Bay proposal bears a strong resemblance to Le Corbusier's plan for Saint-Dié, but adapted and made practical for American conditions. As at Saint-Dié, the central group of buildings is on a raised podium, is dominated by a single office tower designed as an elongated hexagon, and faces an auditorium with a distinctive exterior shape. Also like Saint-Dié, the external spaces are created by large horizontal building masses. The principal differences are that the podium is a garage for five thousand cars, there is a large internal shopping center, and the scale of the external spaces is modulated by smaller, lower buildings, as at Lijnbaan. This design, although it resembles only slightly the Prudential Center designed by Charles Luckman, which was ultimately built on the site, helped to define the image of desirable urban renewal, and was mirrored in hundreds of projects in other cities.

Victor Gruen was commissioned to develop the Fort Worth plan as a result of an article he had written for the *Harvard Business Review* on the applicability of regional shopping center designs to the revitalization of existing downtowns. Gruen had already been the architect for two prototypical shopping centers: Northland in suburban Detroit, and Southdale in suburban Minneapolis. The Fort Worth plan suggested that the expressway system form a ring around the business center, rather than cut through it. Within the ring, parking garages would intercept traffic and streets within the entire central district would become pedestrian precincts—with no point less than a six-minute walk from one of the garages. The buildings downtown would be a mixture of existing structures and new buildings, some of the groups of new structures resembling the Back Bay plan. A pedestrian bridge system between buildings formed a supplemental pedestrian network.

While most of the Fort Worth plan was never carried out, the image of peripheral highway and pedestrian precinct became influential, and the concept of the downtown mall to help the urban retail district compete with suburban shopping centers was to become an almost axiomatic part of modern city design.

Implementation of urban renewal in city centers proved to be a slow process, in which the original design often changed beyond recognition between the initial concept and completion of the actual structures. Often the original design idea was lost completely, and each individual renewal parcel seemed to have a separate, unrelated character. The Boston Government Center, based on an urban design plan by Kevin Lynch and developed further by I. M. Pei and Partners, was one renewal project that retained some of its original design character. A traditional monumental plaza on a large scale, with a state office building playing the role of the bell tower, it had a strong enough character to transcend differences in the design of individual buildings between concept and execution. The Embarcadero Center in San Francisco also retained important features of its original concept, including a common raised plaza level that extended over many blocks and was connected by bridges. Penn Center in Philadelphia, built in place of the old "Chinese Wall" of railway tracks which divided the western portion of the city center, did not follow the original design plan proposed by the City Planning Department, which set forth a series of three parallel office towers not unlike the arrangement of the

Hötorget or the towers of the Lijnbaan. The influence of the city government did at least get the railway land developed as a single parcel, although without the original design clarity—unlike railway land north of Grand Central station in New York City, which was redeveloped on a site-by-site basis after World War II.

One of the largest central-city redevelopments to be carried out in anything like its originally designed form is the Barbican district of the City of London. Designed by the architectural partnership formed by Peter Chamberlin, Geoffrey Powell and Christoph Bon, it sought to unite the modernism and tall buildings of the Hötorget district with traditional British planning concepts like the row house and crescent and the college quadrangle.

Implicit in most modernist city designs from the Ville Contemporaine onward was the belief that the entire existing city should be replaced by an environment in which individual buildings were far more separate than they had been before. It is thus not surprising that the most usual effect of modern city design concepts has been to fragment development and to set up conflicts between new buildings and the preexisting city. Groups of subsidized housing have tended to be located in accordance with the tower-in-park principle, separating them from the surrounding urban context. Most urban renewal plans have been carried out parcel by parcel, with relatively little design continuity among the buildings, and the placement of each building has often been determined by abstract geometric arrangements set in the midst of open space. Zoning ordinances enforce fragmentation on individual developments by giving open space at ground level and setbacks primacy over relationships to streets and surrounding buildings.

To learn what a completely modern city is like we can turn to Chandigarh and Brasilia, both built as new communities under the strong influence of Le Corbusier.

Chandigarh was originally to be designed by Albert Mayer and Matthew Nowicki, but Nowicki was killed in a plane crash in 1950, before the designs for the city had been more than just begun. The government of the Punjab went to Maxwell Fry and Jane Drew to ask them to assume Nowicki's role as architect for their new capital. Fry and Drew suggested that they also bring in Le Corbusier, who in turn brought in his cousin Pierre Jeanneret. Fry, Drew, Jeanneret and Le Corbusier met in India in

1951, and before Albert Mayer arrived, Le Corbusier took Mayer's plan, which was a relatively loosely drawn garden-city concept, and transformed it into something much more closely resembling his Ville Radieuse proposal of 1935.

According to Maxwell Fry, Mayer was not fluent in French, so Le Corbusier ignored him completely when he did arrive at the working meeting. Mayer had placed the capitol in a park at the northeast corner of the site; Le Corbusier pulled it to the center of the north side of the city, squarely on a monumental axis. Mayer's plan had two parkways running north-south, flanking the business center, and a large number of gently curving streets; Le Corbusier converted the plan to a sector system with a large rectangular grid. Again, according to Fry, Le Corbusier sketched out his new design on the analogy of the human body, calling the capitol the head, the business center the stomach, and so on, suggesting that a similar process of thought went into the Ville Radieuse plan, which seems to have a head, shoulders, a torso and legs.

Enough of the original garden-city concept remains that a visitor to Chandigarh is more conscious of the landscaping of the principal streets than of the generally mediocre buildings. Le Corbusier's real mark as a designer has been as the architect of the capitol complex. The secretariat, legislative and court buildings have been completed, but, at least partly because the governor's palace was never built, the grouping of structures is separated by distances too large to permit them to read as an ensemble. The fragmentation that characterized modernist intervention in existing cities thus is also present at Chandigarh.

The concept for Brasilia is essentially the work of two architects who were both heavily influenced by Le Corbusier: Lucio Costa, who completed the initial master plan in 1957, and Oscar Niemeyer, who has designed most of the significant buildings and prepared design controls for other development. The key element of the plan for Brasilia is the central highway, which forms a symmetrical, bow-shaped curve across a broad plain and becomes the spine for a series of sectors. These sectors are rigidly zoned to separate different types of land uses. Some contain widely spaced residential blocks like those suggested by Le Corbusier at Saint-Dié, with the buildings up off the ground plane and surrounded by open space. The capitol district is at the center point of the highway curve; in plan it looks rather like the fusilage and swept-back wings of an airplane. Beyond a greenbelt, winding roads lead to apartment towers located in the surrounding hills.

Brasilia does have some of the design consistency of one of Le Corbusier's visionary drawings. Tall buildings of similar size and shape are placed in a regular pattern and set in sweeping areas of open space. The automobile is the major means of communication. The result has been called empty and soulless, and while it may be premature to arrive at a definitive judgment of a community that has been begun so recently, Brasilia does seem to present significant proof that the modernist city formulation leaves out some of the essentials of a vital urban area.

The tall building and the expressway, as Le Corbusier foresaw, are the two most significant elements of the modern city. But rather than acting as design determinants, they have usually been constructed without any controlling concept of city design whatever. Highway planning, slum clearance and urban renewal have nevertheless embodied an attitude that Le Corbusier prefigured in his city plans, a sense that radical changes in the city were necessary and that they could and should be decided by technicians on behalf of the rest of the people. This authoritarian attitude and a certain contempt for the existing urban structure were implicit in the design of urban highways and urban renewal projects that required the total clearance of large parts of the existing city.

A reaction to the modernist city began in the 1960s, just at the time when modernist concepts of city design were making their mark on almost every urban area in the world. The demand for community participation, a renewed interest in historic preservation and the beginnings of the environmental movement helped create a need for smaller-scale proposals and an appreciation of the virtues of the monumental and garden-city design concepts. At the same time, a different perception of the inadequacies of the modern city led to an interest in city design that would be more comprehensive and more authoritarian, and that would produce nothing less than the complete transformation of urban life. This alternative is the subject of the next chapter.

91: Tall buildings made possible by the elevator and steel frame created an unprecedented design problem. At first, architects left the rear walls and party walls of tall buildings without architectural treatment. Even Louis Sullivan, often considered a preeminent theorist of skyscraper design, did not realize that tall buildings required space around them, and cities would not be built up uniformly to the new height. The cartoonist for the American *Architectural Review* in 1904 was probably more concerned with stylistic variety as a city-design problem but aptly captured the problems of height as well.

92: Le Corbusier shows in this all-too-prophetic drawing, made in the early 1920s, that he did understand that tall buildings require space around them and was willing to take this idea to its logical conclusion. Individual tall buildings stand in isolation along an elevated highway, all the same size and of the same design.

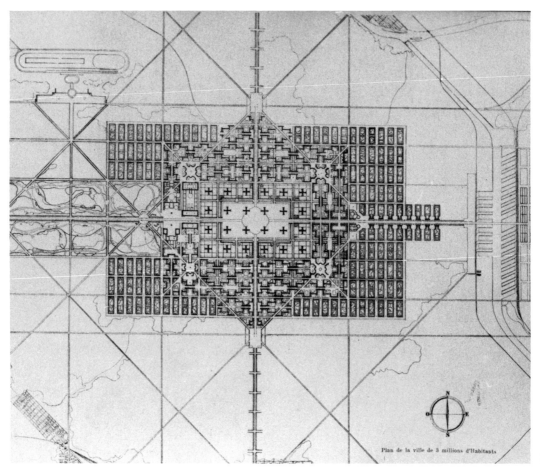

Plan de la ville de 3 millions d'Habitants

93: Le Corbusier's 1922 design for a city of three million people organizes tall buildings within a rigid geometrical system. The managerial elite were to live near the downtown skyscrapers; satellite towns for workers and their factories would be built beyond the greenbelt.

94: Le Corbusier's 1925 Voisin Plan for Paris obliterates the historic center of the city in favor of a rigid system of tall office buildings and large apartment complexes, with a limited-access highway seen plowing through the city, long before such highways were actually constructed. Note that uniform height and architecture plus a powerful geometrical organization give this design a coherence and order which turned out to be difficult to obtain when city reconstruction on this pattern was attempted after World War II.

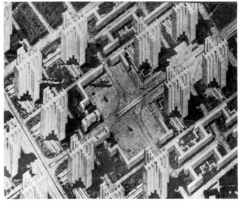

95: This set of drawings by Harvey Corbett, from the New York City Regional Plan of 1929, shows a city street evolving into a multilevel system in which pedestrian and automobile traffic would be separated. Unlike Le Corbusier's Voisin Plan, the modernization of the city could be a gradual process.

96

96: A parallel alternative to the Voisin Plan approach to tall building design can be see in this drawing, also from the Regional Plan for New York City, in which large office towers are separated from each other but remain set within the context of a complex city, and each tower is assumed to have a different designer and developer.

97, 98, 99: Hugh Ferris's ideas for *The Metropolis of Tomorrow,* also published in 1929, were derived in part from New York City's zoning laws and current development practice. He, too, imagined clusters of towers separated by low buildings on a regular system. The city plan is divided into three segments, devoted to business, science and culture. Great avenues flow under the major buildings, with local traffic on the streets and pedestrian bridges above.

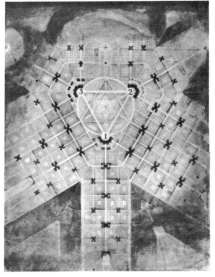

98

100

101

100: Modernism for low-income housing was in large part a question of freeing people from the dank courtyards and air shafts that had characterized much of the nineteenth-century workers' housing constructed by real estate speculators. This drawing of workmen's houses, from Tony Garnier's *Cité Industrielle,* was used to illustrate Le Corbusier's *Towards a New Architecture.*

101: "La Cité Moderne," built in Brussels in 1921–1922, may have been the first urban district actually constructed where the concept of modernism was part of the design program. The architect was Victor Bourgeois.

102

102: The Weissenhof Housing Settlement, planned by the Deutscher Werkbund for the city of Stuttgart and opened in 1927, was a demonstration project that, under the direction of Mies van der Rohe, was to show an environment created of buildings appropriate to the modern age. The participants managed to adopt a coordinated architectural vocabulary, but the site plan looks almost accidental, showing that Mies as the site planner and his colleagues put much more store in uniformity of architectural expression than in coherent city design.

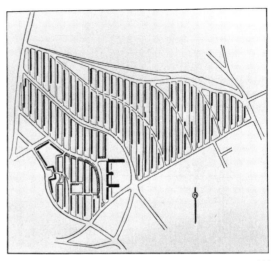

103, 104: This design for housing at Rothenberg by Otto Haesler was presented in a model that dominated the housing section of the 1932 Museum of Modern Art exhibition on modern architecture. Haesler favored long parallel rows of buildings, so that each apartment could have an optimal orientation.

105, 106: Hendrik Berlage's first plan for the Amsterdam South district of 1902 was revised by him four years after his 1911 visit to Chicago, where Berlage would have seen the Burnham plan with its large-scale road network.

107: Buildings by the architects of the Amsterdam school that implemented Berlage's plan used the familiar street and courtyard with generous open space and gardens, and an architectural vocabulary based on a somewhat whimsical interpretation of folk traditions. The housing in this example is by G. J. Rutgers.

108

108: A section of a planned district in Berlin, designed by Bruno Taut. Neglected by Sigfried Giedion and other formulators of the Modern Movement concept in architecture, Taut was one of the most accomplished architects and urban designers to work in what has been considered the modernist vernacular.

109: The Karl Marx Hof, a building for 1,500 families, designed by Karl Ehn and completed in 1930, is the best-known workers' housing built in Vienna in the interwar period; its courtyard plans and long facades were representative of government-supported housing in Vienna.

109

110: Housing at China Walk, Lambeth. The high-density housing built by the London County Council during the interwar period was designed in a collegiate Georgian style that seems to have rendered it invisible to proponents of modern architecture. These buildings nevertheless used modern building construction and modern standards of light and air, with site plans that created urbane street facades and courtyards.

111: Housing at Villeurbanne, near Lyon, designed by M. Leroux and completed in 1934, was one of the few housing developments in Europe during the interwar period where the tall building was an important element.

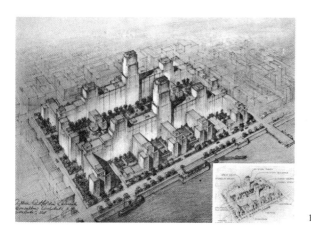

112: The courtyard-type organization for housing was studied in this diagram by Arthur Holden for the New York City Regional Plan, and, 113, 114 was adopted by Clarence Stein for his 1933 design for Hillside Homes, built in the Bronx with subsidies from a New York State program, the design based partly on Stein's earlier Phipps garden apartments.

112

113

114

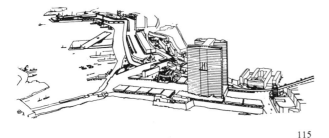

115: The attitudes that were to shape post–World War II reconstruction and development were already well established in the interwar period. Le Corbusier himself called his first plan for Algiers in 1930 an artillery shell that would shatter current notions of the city. The drawing shows a quasi-official plan for Algiers that Le Corbusier made in 1937, which would have been only marginally less shattering. Among other proposals, the plan sought to decant the business district into a single large building.

115

116: Le Corbusier's 1937 plan for Buenos Aires would also have required radical changes in the city. A new business center would be constructed on an island in the harbor; the whole waterfront would be redeveloped; expressways would overlay the existing street system and divide the city into sectors; subdistricts would be completely redeveloped, with buildings on a new, larger scale. All the ingredients of what was later to be called urban renewal are present in this proposal.

116

117, 118: These photomontages, presentations of buildings proposed by Ludwig Mies van der Rohe in the 1920s, were meant to show these designs as desirable improvements to the city. Today they can be read as prophecies of the disruptive effect on cities of buildings that asserted their modernity at the expense of existing city-design elements such as continuity of materials and planned height relationships.

117

118

119: Photograph of the model "The World of 1960," designed by Norman Bel Geddes for the General Motors Pavilion of the New York World's Fair of 1939. Bel Geddes followed Ferris and other designers in separating the tall buildings more widely than the real estate market turned out to prefer, and in underrating the potential decay of older areas; otherwise his prediction was astonishingly accurate.

120: This rendering by Peter Shepheard from the 1944 *Greater London Plan* shows the influence of Swedish concepts of city design, a more domestic and "sensible" version of European modernism that had gone on being built in Sweden while the rest of Europe went through World War II.

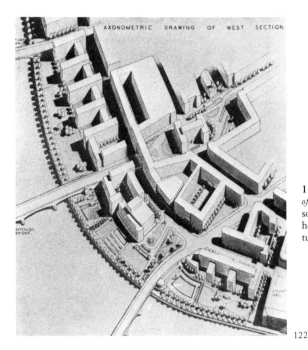

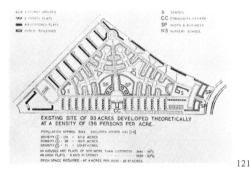

121: This neighborhood diagram, from the 1943 *County of London Plan,* and the axonometric drawing, 122, of the south bank of the Thames from the same document show how city designers saw wartime devastation as an opportunity to modernize London.

123, 124: Stockholm's Hötorget district was one of the
first places where second-level pedestrian walkways were
actually constructed. Unlike Harvey Corbett's studies for
the Regional Plan Association, the plan shows the street
itself also given to pedestrians, with traffic deflected
around the district.

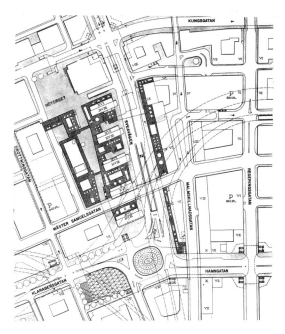

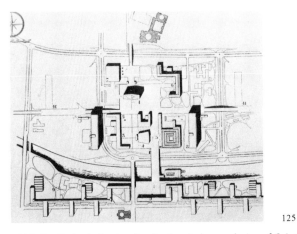

125

125: Le Corbusier's plan for the bomb-damaged city of Saint-Dié started over again completely, and influenced many post–World War II renewal plans, including this plan, 126, for Boston, Massachusetts, drawn by a team that included Walter Gropius.

126

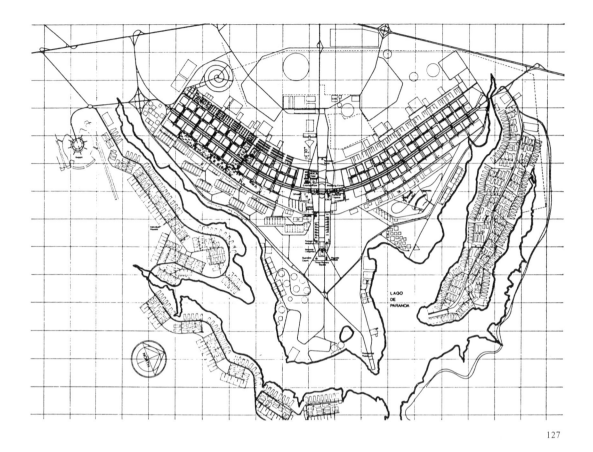

127

127, 128: Brasilia is perhaps the prototypical modern city, the place where Le Corbusier's city-design ideas came closest to implementation. Brasilia made it obvious to all that the city-design theories advocated by C.I.A.M. were based on an oversimplification of the nature of cities. There is more to city design than light and air for apartments, an efficient traffic network, and a logical zoning system.

128

129

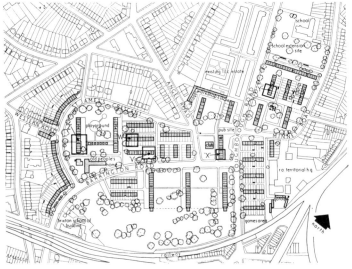

129, 130: The Loughborough Road housing estate in the London borough of Lambeth shows the strong influence of Le Corbusier's ideas on official design in England during the 1950s. This plan was prepared by the L.C.C. Architect's department under, successively, Robert Matthew and Leslie Martin. Colin St. John Wilson and Alan Colquhoun were among the young staff architects who worked on this project.

130

131: The reconstruction of the Barbican district, a heavily bombed area in the City of London, was begun in the 1950s but not brought to completion for more than twenty years. The introduction of residential buildings into what had been primarily a financial district is an attempt to create a more self-contained "24-hour city," and counteract the vast geographical spread and consequent long commuting distances of the modern metropolis. The 1959 plan for the Barbican by Chamberlin, Powell & Bon has a basic arrangement inspired by collegiate quadrangles. The three towers are shown covered with a patterned grille.

132: Victor Gruen's 1956 plan for Fort Worth took the principle of the Hötorget to a much larger scale, diverting traffic around the entire central business district and making all of downtown a pedestrian precinct.

133: The Houston skyline in 1984: closer to the 1929 New York Regional Plan than to Le Corbusier's vision of a Ville Contemporaine. Each major development turns out to require its own distinctive architectural image, and the idiosyncrasies of the real estate market make it unlikely that towers can be regularly spaced or of similar size.

134: This drawing by Lee Copeland is part of a 1974 plan for a downtown district of Seattle, in which a boulevard street is shown in a modernist idiom. The tower in the park and the apartment block located for its most favorable orientation have been set aside in favor of more traditional urban values.

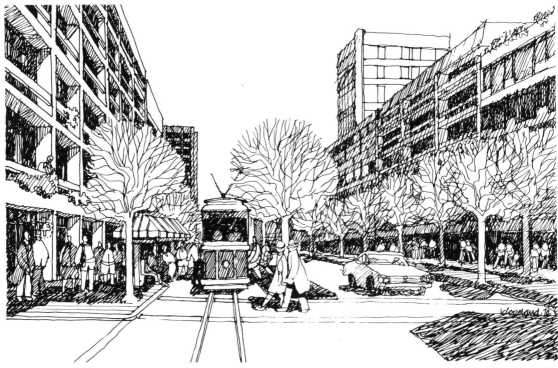

5

Megastructures: The City as a Building

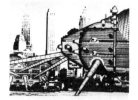

From the mid 1950s, and for almost twenty years, the idea of an urban area as a large, interconnected building dominated much architectural thinking about cities. The street would become a weather-protected corridor or bridge, the plaza an interior atrium, the building an incident within a larger framework. The idea seemed to appeal especially to designers in Great Britain and Japan, but it soon became widely accepted all over the world.

Recent visions of the city as a gigantic structure were almost always tied to a future in which the imperfections of modern cities would be swept away by the force of new technology. However, the idea of the city as an enormous building was actually a well-established concept that went back to the royal palace, which was always a self-contained community within a city, and sometimes in preindustrial times assumed the dimensions of the city itself.

When Roman imperial power declined, the palace that the emperor Diocletian had built in the early fourth century A.D. on what is now the Yugoslavian coast was taken over by the people of the area and served them as an entire walled city; it is now about half the historic center of the modern city of Split.

Diocletian's palace was designed according to the plan of a Roman military camp, which had been the basis for the plan of many cities from Pompeii to what is now the core of modern Florence. Diocletian built a rectangular walled enclosure with gates in the center of each elevation. The two main streets ran straight from the gates and intersected at the center. The emperor's living quarters were along one of the short walls, facing the Mediterranean. The rest of the complex was organized around

157

four courtyards, one in each of the quadrants formed by the intersecting streets.

During the Baroque period the centralization of royal power produced building programs comparable in scale to those of the Roman emperors. Versailles itself, although a landmark of monumental design thinking, is also clearly the palace as city, with members of the court and their dependents living in the building complex for years at a time.

The enormous, foursquare royal palace at Caserta, near Naples, designed by Luigi Vanvitelli, was begun in 1752 and finished in 1774. The building and its courtyards cover an area of about twelve acres, making it slightly larger than Diocletian's palace. Caserta is not fortified and its extensive gardens carry the palace's architectural organization into the surrounding landscape, making it seem even larger. According to George Hersey, the design of Caserta was probably influenced by the tradition of reconstructions of King Solomon's Temple, often portrayed as a massive, symmetrical palace big enough to house a huge court and all its thousands of retainers.

Versailles had grown as the ambitions of the king and court increased, so that not all the various architectural elements of the palace were in scale with each other when the building reached its ultimate extension. Compared with rigidly symmetrical Caserta and other late Baroque palaces, Versailles began to look a little bit improvised. In 1780 the director of royal buildings commissioned Etienne-Louis Boullée to redesign Versailles. Boullée's design in effect created a whole new building ensemble in front of the existing palace. It was a hierarchical organization of five buildings, each itself the size of an enormous palace. The project was far too expensive even for the French royal court. That it was contemplated at all shows how completely the nobility at the court of Louis XVI misjudged the political situation that was to lead to the revolution and the execution of the king.

This design seems, however, to have unlocked in Boullée an interest in architecture on an enormous scale, a scale far more grandiose than that at Versailles. His projects from the 1780s and 1790s include gigantic architectural arrangements not unlike Diocletian's palace in organization. The Municipal Palace of 1792 shows an enormous building contained within massive walls, with four internal precincts defined by two intersecting interior ways.

An idealized palace design became associated with some social-reform concepts in the late eighteenth and early nineteenth centuries. Jeremy Bentham's panopticon, in Bentham's view equally well adapted to a prison or a poorhouse, is an example. A circular or octagonal plan is connected to a central control point by radiating streetlike corridors. Where Robert Owen saw the village as the key image of a society of unity and mutual cooperation, the French philosopher François-Marie-Charles Fourier chose the palace as the image of his phalanstery, a communal living environment for 1,600 to 1,800 people. A Versailles-like ensemble of buildings was to be designed for ordinary people supporting themselves, not working in the service of a king. Fourier captioned the drawing of his phalanstery with the phrase "L'Avenir"; perhaps for the first time, the idea of a city as a building was combined with the idea of a society that would become perfectible in the future.

The city as building began to become associated within the use of new technology during the last half of the nineteenth century. Two of the first technologies that were to suggest development ideas on the scale of the city were greenhouse structures made entirely of metal and glass, and the streetcar, which was easier to incorporate into city design than the steam-driven railroad train.

Metal and glass were the materials for the Crystal Palace that was constructed in London's Hyde Park for the Great Exposition of 1851. It was a greatly enlarged version of the greenhouses, train sheds and shopping arcades that its architect, Joseph Paxton, and others had already designed from cast-iron frameworks and large panes of glass. However, the scale of the Crystal Palace and the speed with which its modular construction was carried out were both something new. It was 1,848 feet long by 408 feet wide; its central transept was 72 feet wide and 108 feet high. The whole structure was one and one-half times as big as Caserta, and it was all built in a little more than half a year. The Crystal Palace is thus an important step in the evolution of the concept of the city as a building. The term "Crystal Palace" was coined not by the architect but by the magazine *Punch,* whose recognition of the palace tradition in a building that was not at all obviously like a palace is significant. Here then was a structure on the scale of an enclosed city street with buildings on both sides, a third of a mile long. Not only was it built in a short time, but its modular parts permitted it to be taken down and rebuilt at Sydenham, southeast of London, when the exhibition in Hyde Park was over.

The idea of a city enclosed by a building, and the concept that the components of such a city might be demountable, were both to become important city-design ideas a century later. The immediate influence of the Crystal Palace seems to have been on shopping arcades and other exhibition buildings. The Galleria Vittorio Emanuele, designed by Giuseppe Mengoni and constructed in Milan in 1865, is a famous example of an enclosed shopping street with a glass roof, a concept that suggests that it could be extended into a system. Shopping arcades of an analogous design were constructed in most major cities.

The influence of the Crystal Palace may also be seen in the project for "Aerodomes" published by the French engineer Henry-Jules Borie in 1865. A system of glassed-in galleries thousands of feet long is surrounded by buildings connected at midheight by pedestrian bridges that establish a secondary means of circulation. The newly invented safety elevator permitted Borie to postulate buildings twice the height of the typical structures of his time. This proposal was intended as a prototype design for the centers of all major cities, where high land values would require a more efficient use of land.

The horse car, the cable car and then the electric streetcar were the means of developing new neighborhoods without the pollution that blighted buildings constructed along railway tracks. Arturo Soria y Mata began advocating the construction of linear cities in 1882, as a logical extension of the streetcar suburb. The key element of Soria's proposal was a wide street with room in the center for trains and streetcars, all utilities, and enough additional land that public buildings could be provided at intervals. Smaller streets would provide access to development on either side of this central spine, and the system would be capable of almost infinite extension. Soria saw linear developments ringing existing cities or stretching across Europe and even to the Orient. An actual linear housing district was constructed according to Soria's principles in the Madrid suburbs starting in 1894, but the scale and density of the development were comparatively modest. The idea of linear cities would later be picked up by Le Corbusier and would ultimately become a component of mid-twentieth-century megastructure designs.

Something like a linear city concept had been suggested by Joseph Paxton as well, in his 1855 proposal for the Great Victorian Way, a circular road that would link all the railroad stations in central London, much as the underground Circle Line was later to do. The road was to have been enclosed by a gigantic glassed-in arcade, flanked by rail lines on either side, with the portion of the arcade between the City and Regent Street forming a linear shopping center. This application of the Crystal Palace concept may well be the origin of the "crystal palace" proposed forty years later by Ebenezer Howard as a linear, circular shopping center at the heart of each garden city.

The Crystal Palace was an innovative structure, but its design was a translation of the traditional church or basilica organization into a new scale and new materials. The drawings made by Antonio Sant'Elia for his Città Nuova project, exhibited in Milan in 1914, sought to translate mechanical innovations into architectural form. Tall, streamlined shapes define a city of rapid travel and technological purity, which owed much to the artifacts of the new industrial society. The most famous drawing shows a railroad station rather like a great dam, with a stream of railway traffic beneath it and clifflike rows of buildings on either side, not the conventional streets and buildings, but what appears to be a city as a single, linear structure.

As Sant'Elia was killed in the First World War, he did not live to see the futurist movement that he had joined absorbed into Mussolini's Fascist ideology. Nor did he ever have to face the implicit problem in a vision of a new order that totally replaces the old: What happens to the old urban fabric and the rights of the city's inhabitants on the way to achieving this vision? It is not absolutely clear that Sant'Elia's future city was intended to replace Milan, but by drawing a completely new urban world, Sant'Elia sought to inspire people to replace existing cities. Le Corbusier's Voisin Plan of 1925 explicitly suggests replacing most of the center of Paris. The difference between modernism and futurism is one of degree. Where the modernist was willing to accept remnants of the past for sentimental reasons, the futurist was more likely to see society totally transformed and all vestiges of the past cast aside in favor of a new kind of environment. The rush to meet the future, as shown in Sant'Elia's drawings, was to become a central element of megastructuralism in the 1960s and 1970s.

The glass and metal of the Crystal Palace or the familiar urban arcade could also be used in the service of a more radical kind of architecture. Just after the First World War, Bruno Taut, who had recently designed the garden community of Falkenberg in Berlin, published his watercolor drawings of *Alpine Architecture,* which go beyond the idea of the city as building to demonstrate the city as landscape. In these elaborate fantasies, mountains were combined with delicate structures of glass and the thinnest possible frames. Taut also wrote a book urging that each city should have a single central structure which would play the dominating role that the cathedral had played in the medieval town, a crowning structure which Taut also believed should be an expressionist building that achieved a crystalline appearance through the use of glass. These design ideas had little immediate influence, nor did they seem to have much effect on Taut's own subsequent development as an architect; but Taut's visionary drawings and writings were to be referred to later by architects of the Archigram Group and other proponents of the city as building during the 1960s.

Buckminster Fuller is another visionary designer who was to be given great attention by megastructuralists during the 1960s and 1970s. Fuller's Dymaxion house, originally designed in 1927, a hexagonal metal building that revolved on a central mast, was the first element in a whole Dymaxion vocabulary meant to accomplish nothing less than the redesign of the entire built environment. Fuller's parallel invention, or rediscovery, of the geodesic dome provided a system that could serve equally well as a small survival structure or, as in one famous project, as the means by which most of Manhattan Island could be turned into an indoor space. During the years when the megastructure was being studied in every architectural school, Fuller's messianic (and marathon) lecturing style made his influence more personal than that of many designers whose ideas circulated only in the form of drawings, photographs and the written word.

In 1929 Raymond Hood made a plan for the development of Manhattan Island which also looks in retrospect like a precursor of ideas that became important in the 1960s. Hood picked up the clusters of towers at major intersections already proposed as a city-design motif in Hugh Ferris's *Metropolis of Tomorrow,* and added to it a series of large bridges lined with massive apartment houses, Of course, the bridge as a street lined with houses was a well-established idea, going back to such structures as the Ponte Vecchio in Florence and old London Bridge. What was new once again was the scale: the bridge structure became an enormous building, with the graduated heights of the apartment towers memorializing the curve of the suspension bridge that presumably was to be the structural concept. The advantage of Hood's bridge proposal is that the rivers were obviously an area of the city that had not been developed and great densities could be added without displacing existing residents. The city as a bridge was a motif that would reemerge later as an important component of the megastructure concept. Hood, however, sought to make his bridge cities look as much like conventional buildings of the time as possible; later bridge-city projects were to make more of the engineering techniques that created the bridges themselves.

In the years after the Second World War, when the present caught up to Le Corbusier's 1920s vision of cities of towers isolated from each other by parkland, another Corbusian vision began to intrigue architects: Le Corbusier's portrayal of whole urban neighborhoods as gigantic buildings.

On his South American trip in 1929, Le Corbusier had made sketches for Rio de Janeiro, São Paulo and Montevideo which showed elevated highways running through each city, with buildings underneath them. This idea was elaborated by Le Corbusier in 1930 in the much better known plan for Algiers, which included an elevated highway whose supporting structure would have provided a framework for 180,000 dwelling units. Le Corbusier continued to revise this concept during the 1930s, and in a later plan for the Algiers business center, added the concept of decanting all business activities into a single, massive office tower. After the war, as described in the previous chapter, Le Corbusier was commissioned to design a residential building on the scale of the Algiers office tower, the Unité d'Habitation.

The Unité—a large apartment house designed to be a self-contained community, with a "street of shops" on an intermediate floor and a kindergarten on the roof—had a tremendous influence on other architects, particularly in Great Britain, where its design affected an entire generation of publicly aided housing. Alison and Peter Smithson's 1952 competition design for housing at Golden Lane in London took Le Corbusier's upper-level street of shops inside an *unité de'habitation* and elaborated it into a concept of streets in the air, interconnecting linear buildings to form a subdistrict of a city.

The street-in-the-air concept, although related to the external access balconies that had often been used in European housing designs, had also acquired a strong symbolic significance derived from other sources than the work of Le Corbusier.

An often reproduced illustration of a future city from the 1908 edition of Moses King's *Views of New York* showed pedestrian bridges linking the tops of office buildings. The 1926 Regional Plan for New York City had explored the possibility of a new pedestrian walkway system, one level above the street. The idea had been taken up by set designers and illustrators and had become a staple of any description of the city of the future.

Le Corbusier's *Vers une Architecture,* originally published in 1923, pointed to structures that new technology made possible, such as ocean liners or grain elevators, to argue for a modern architecture and against the historical styles. A new generation of industrial artifacts had begun to interest architects after the Second World War: petroleum refineries and cracking plants with their acres and acres of complex piping, offshore platforms, giant dams that transform entire landscapes, and rockets capable of space travel.

The possibility of space travel in particular gave a whole new meaning to futurism, and architects began to look with interest at science fiction books and comics with illustrations of space colonies and the cities of "advanced civilizations" from other planets, which had in turn been strongly influenced by Buckminster Fuller and by the work of industrial designers like Raymond Loewy, who had sought futuristic imagery for industrial products.

It was from such diverse sources as Le Corbusier's cities as buildings, new industrial artifacts, and science fiction illustrations, as well as greenhouse and arcade traditions and linear city plans, that ideas were to coalesce suddenly into the megastructure movement. The most serious interest in the city as building seems to have been generated in places where buildable land was scarce, like Japan and England. The Japanese architect Kenzo Tange's first megastructure project was done with M.I.T. students for Boston Harbor in 1959. The next year saw the publication of Tange's similar plan for Tokyo Bay, which took two highways carried on huge suspension bridges across the water. Between the two highways was to be a long, densely populated island which would contain the commercial center of the new city, while at right angles to the highways were causeways leading to residential structures created by huge slanting buildings back to back, like Japanese temple roofs on a gigantic scale.

Metabolism 1960—A Proposal for a New Urbanism was published in connection with the 1960 World Design Conference in Tokyo. The authors were the architects Kiyonoru Kikutake, Masato Otaka, Fumihiko Maki and Kisho Kurokawa, and the graphic designer Kiyoshi Awazu. The Metabolist theory postulated cities designed to grow and change with time and different conditions. The underlying structure would be permanent, but units of the city would be attached to the structure as flowers to a stalk or leaves to a tree.

Kikutake made a series of projects of cylindrical residential towers built over water from 1958 to 1962, of which his "Ocean City" project, with collars of bug-eyed apartment units surrounding cylindrical concrete support shafts, is the most remembered image.

Kurokawa prepared a concept for an agricultural city at the invitation of the Museum of Modern Art in New York City, and the project was exhibited there in 1961. This city was a grid suspended from towers a story above the ground, in theory leaving valuable agricultural land undisturbed.

A City in the Sky, following a somewhat similar design, was developed by Arata Isozaki between 1960 and 1962. Isozaki was not a participant in the formulation of the Metabolist concept, but he had worked for Tange and knew the Metabolists. His best-remembered presentation drawing of his City in the Sky shows cylindrical concrete towers supporting bridgelike buildings that span between them. This concept is shown in collage over a photograph of a ruined Greek temple, with the cylindrical towers—which should certainly be something like one hundred feet high—drawn so that they are the same size as individual ruined columns, which clearly must be much smaller. In the foreground is an elevated highway, and what seems to be a ruined bridgelike structure, which has fallen from one of the concrete supports—or alternatively is under construction and has yet to be hoisted into place.

Whatever Isozaki intended by this drawing is protected by so many layers of irony that it remains obscure. Is this a serious proposal comparable to the cities as space-frame trusses being drawn by Yona Friedman in France at the same period? Other drawings and an elaborate model are testimony that Isozaki was indeed seriously developing this idea. Is this particular drawing a commentary on the triumph of modern technology over ancient civilization or is it meant to indicate that all structures and cities are similar and will meet the same fate?

In any event, the idea that new cities could be built over old, and that they would take the form of a permanent system that supports adjustable and temporary units, became a major ingredient in the development of city designs as buildings.

A permanent supporting structure combined with relatively temporary capsules, which can be plugged into one location and later moved to another, lies behind much of the work of the Archigram Group, which started at London's Architectural Association School when most of its members were still students and began publishing their own magazine during 1961. The Archigram program was not so much to create the city of the future as to shake up the British architectural establishment. They wanted their readers to look at Bruno Taut's expressionistic Alpine architecture, at Buckminster Fuller's domes and capsules, at Fuller associate James Fitzgibbon's 1960 circular city on the water, as well as at the cities envisioned in space comics and illustrating stories in science fiction magazines. *Archigram 4* takes its readers on a tour of cities portrayed in space comics: "A respectful salute in the general direction of Roy Lichtenstein and we're off . . ."

Some of the best-known city images created by Archigram Group members themselves include the Interchange Project of 1963 by Ron Herron and Warren Chalk, Peter Cook's Plug-In City of 1964, and Ron Herron's Walking City, also of 1964.

Herron and Chalk's urban interchange is a building in the shape of a flattened sphere where monorails, vehicles running along highways on guides, and railroads meet. The interchange is connected by long, telescoping tubes that contain moving sidewalks to surrounding cylindrical towers, which resemble the vacuum tubes that were used in radio receivers in the days before transistors.

The principal Plug-In City drawing was an enormous axonometric that showed an agglomeration of cylindrical towers, inverted pyramids of plug-in, modular housing, and linear stepped-back terraces of housing, all served by tubular connectors. At the edge of the city giant hovercraft, drawn as cylindrical buildings, provided a regional transportation link. The whole composition was deliberately irregular, to suggest that building on this scale did not necessarily mean a regimented environment.

The plug-in concept was meant to be a method of permitting structures to be tailored to the needs of individuals, with endless permutations creating cities of infinite variety. As drawn, however, their high densities and complex interdependent structures would have required an unprecedented degree of social regimentation.

Plug-In City was worked out to show, among other details, how cranes at the top of structural frames would lift capsules into place, how services operated, and the way balloons could be inflated to seal off bad weather. One drawing, made to resemble a weather map, showed England as a series of high- and low-pressure development zones, with Plug-In City eventually filling in all the high-pressure zones.

Walking City was an arresting image of ovoid megastructures on huge telescoping legs. While the individual parts of the megastructure have an architectural character, the overall effect is of gigantic insectile creatures. There was always an element of jokiness in Archigram proposals, no matter how serious its proponents actually were about the main points they were making. The drawing "The Walking City in New York," by which the Walking City proposal is generally known, has more jokiness than usual. It shows the Walking City buildings arriving in New York harbor, with the Manhattan skyline in the background. Even if you are willing to accept the idea of sixty-story buildings moving on gigantic legs, it is hard to believe they can walk on water.

As the decade of the 1960s continued, the work of the Archigram group became more ecologically minded, more interested in underground cities, and at the same time more involved with demountable structures and environments for entertainment.

An interest in ecology is supposedly the motivating force behind a series of projects by Paolo Soleri, dating from 1959 and continuing through the 1960s, for huge underground, spherical or tower cities that would concentrate population and urban activities to protect the landscape. Soleri, a graduate of the École des Beaux Arts during its last days who also spent some months studying with Frank Lloyd Wright at Taliesin, is able to combine monumental architectural compositions in the tradition of Boullée with the kind of "organic" engineering that Wright had used for the S. C. Johnson and Son administration building: forms in reinforced concrete that appear to have been designed by analogy with plants.

Soleri began construction on Arcosanti, a prototype for a megastructural city, in the Arizona desert in 1970. Progress has proceeded by slow, craft methods, mostly with volunteer student labor, and to date has achieved nothing beyond the scale of a small village. Soleri alone of the megastructuralists of the 1960s seems to have retained an unbroken faith in the concept, and the gap between his visions and their realization does not seem to deter him. Another powerful megastructure image is the space-frame drawn by Yona Friedman, in studies dating from 1960, to spread over existing cities. The idea is that existing urban activities would be drawn up into the space-frame, and the outmoded and now disused structures at ground level could later be demolished.

Hans Hollein's aircraft carrier projects of 1964 took the final steps toward relating Le Corbusier's polemic in favor of engineering imagery for architecture to a program for city design. Where Le Corbusier urged the ocean liner as an example of a new architecture already achieved, Hollein constructed collages showing aircraft carriers on dry land or buried in the landscape to demonstrate that habitable structures at the scale of the city already existed.

By the mid-1960s the idea of the city as a building began to have a visible effect on actual structures. Kenzo Tange's Yamanishi Communications Center at Kofu, finished in 1967, has a strong resemblance to Isozaki's City in the Sky drawing of cylindrical towers supporting bridge-like structures, although, as Reyner Banham noted, Tange's building "is really a monolithic statue commemorating an ideal of adaptability that was practically impossible to realize in built fact."

Expo 1967, the world's fair held in Montreal, was the first occasion for a large public to see megastructural city-design ideas in built form. Perhaps the best-known component of this exhibition was Habitat, the housing project designed by Moshe Safdie. Habitat consisted of prefabricated concrete apartment capsules that were hoisted into position on a reinforced-concrete armature. The capsules were neither standardized nor removable; as they helped support each other, an apartment near the bottom needed quite a different wall structure from one at the top of the eleven-story complex. The resulting building had some of the picturesque qualities of a Mediterranean hilltop village blended with the promise of new technology, a potent combination. The high cost and idiosyncratic character of Habitat was to deny it the prototypical influence that Safdie had hoped for it.

The Place Bonaventure, which was completed in Montreal the year of Expo, has megastructural characteristics, although from the outside it appeared only to be a very large building. Built over railway tracks and a connection to the metro system, it had a shopping concourse, a convention hall of more than 200,000 square feet, six floors of merchandise mart and then a hotel built around courtyards at the top of the structure. The exterior of the Place Bonaventure showed the influence of Paul Rudolph's architecture and art studio building at Yale, completed in 1964. It, in turn, can be compared with megastructures like those from the central portion of Kenzo Tange's Tokyo Bay project. Each tower of the Rudolph building, actually only the size of a small classroom, can be read as a scaled-down version of a massive separate building, with the bridges between them the size of whole town centers.

Rudolph used megastructure imagery in other buildings, such as the Boston Government Center designed in 1963, which contains elevated bridgelike elements; and the campus of the Southern Massachusetts Institute of Technology, which was designed the same year and, as a group of similar elements in a linear arrangement, effectively was a megastructure. Rudolph also designed several megastructure projects on an even larger scale, including, in 1967, a graphic arts center and housing in lower Manhattan, which was meant to be built of prefabricated apartment elements similar to mobile home units; and a continuous residential structure to be built over the then proposed lower Manhattan expressway, also designed in 1967.

Some large housing developments of the period were actually built as megastructures. The Byker estate at Newcastle in the north of England, by the Anglo-Swedish architect Ralph Erskine, was the largest of several continuous structures that Erskine designed with one elevation almost blank and the other opening out generously with windows and balconies. Originally devised to ward off north winds, this design in Newcastle screens the housing from an adjacent highway. The whole complex was planned to be almost a mile long.

The Brunswick Centre in London, with its Sant'Elia-like towers, was a housing project for the Camden Borough Council designed by Leslie Martin and Patrick Hodgkinson. It is like a megastructure because its architectural arrangement is capable of infinite extension: two parallel rows of buildings, designed in a terraced or stadium section, with a shopping concourse and garage in between.

Because the 1960s and early 1970s were a period of great expansion for colleges and universities, there were many opportunities to design a whole new campus or large groups of college buildings. Some of these new colleges were housed in megastructures, notably Scarborough College near Toronto by John Andrews, with its almost industrial silhouette, and Simon Fraser University at Burnaby, British Columbia, by Arthur Erickson, with its internal street covered by a space-frame.

It can be argued that many large regional shopping centers are in fact megastructures, descended both from the Crystal Palace urban arcade tradition and from the internal controlled environment of megastructure projects, with the storefronts representing something like the interchangeable plug-in elements suggested by Archigram.

The large international airports built since the 1960s often have megastructural characteristics, as they house a large, self-contained, if somewhat limited community. Sometimes the architects have emphasized the likeness, as at the terminal building of Charles de Gaulle Airport near Paris, where inclined tubes connecting across a central circular space clearly owe some of their inspiration to Ron Herron and Warren Chalk's Archigram Interchange project.

The Archigram aesthetic of bridgelike structures, much visible piping, and articulation of space into capsules also influenced Renzo Piano and Richard Rogers' 1970 winning competition design for the Centre Pompidou in Paris and carried over into the completed building.

The Expo 1970 world's fair in Osaka—a festive array of space-frames, capsules and robots—marked a kind of climax for the megastructure movement. Also in 1970, Kenzo Tange published a plan that treated the entire Japanese archipelago as a megastructure. By 1972 the Nakagin Capsule Tower by Kisho Kurokawa was completed in Tokyo. Extremely compact prefabricated living units, looking like elongated clothes dryers, were attached to concrete towers. Here was a plug-in structure actually completed. But the Nakagin tower was not a precursor of plug-in cities; it was an isolated and idiosyncratic building. By 1972 the whole idea of the city as a megastructure was in decline almost everywhere.

The megastructure as a vision of an entire future city had never overcome awkward practical problems. Most city development is financed in increments over time; it is rarely practical to build structures for hundreds of thousands of people in just a few years. If such an undertaking is to be privately financed, the real-estate market will not absorb so much new development; if government-supported, the municipal power to finance needs to be spread over a larger period of time, and the political problems of governmental projects increase geometrically with size.

The structural framework of a megastructure is also a new element that is not required by conventional buildings; it is needed to hold up the equivalent of conventional buildings that will be built at a later time. The real-estate market is not accustomed to financing the non-income-producing cylindrical towers or mile-square space-frames that can receive individual dwelling capsules at some time in the future. Rai Okamoto's urban design plan for midtown Manhattan, proposed by the Regional Plan Association in 1969, ran aground on this problem. The concept was to control new growth by causing future buildings to be constructed in clusters. To make the clusters happen, elevators, fire stairs, vertical ductwork and other service elements for future buildings would be constructed first. But the question of who would pay was never answered.

Many megastructure concepts were based on the assumption that people should be able to move their complete house or office from one location to another. It is usually more flexible, however, for people to simply move their belongings to another space, whose location and size are more suitable for their current needs.

The only strong argument in favor of the future city as a gigantic building was that it represented an orderly and efficient means of growth. But taking the order and efficiency of a building up to the scale of a city can actually create enormous inefficiencies. The notorious Pruitt-Igoe housing development in St. Louis, which was so unsuccessful that parts of it were ultimately dynamited, was built in 1955 on something like a megastructure scale (2,764 apartments), and with access galleries for the apartments that were a version of the street-in-the-air concept of Le Corbusier. The problems with Pruitt-Igoe may well have been administrative as well as architectural, as projects of comparable size and similar design have been more successful in other cities, but it illustrates the dangers of large projects where the individual dwelling really is an anonymous capsule in a large, impersonal framework. Pruitt-Igoe became an important symbol for those who questioned the assumptions that lay behind much of the enthusiasm for megastructures.

One of these assumptions was that cities were centralized and congested. But the 1960s and 1970s were the period when the automobile and the truck created the enormous extension of cities and the decentralization of many functions that had once existed only in the congested downtown area. These trends had begun before the Second World War but had been interrupted by economic depression and then the war itself.

The new pattern came about more quickly in North America and Australia than in Europe or Japan, but it was visible everywhere. The automobile made many of the previous requirements for urban concentration irrelevant, and—by removing industry from the city center—had set the stage for the re-creation of the center as a preserve for business, tourism and high-income residents.

A primary purpose of the megastructure was to create a vast increase in density within the confines of the existing city. But by the 1960s and 1970s many people neither needed nor wanted to live at this kind of density.

The 1970s also saw the replacement of old ideas about the advantages of rapid growth and large-scale urban development with ideals that came close to being the opposite. Jane Jacobs has stood Daniel Burnham's famous axiom on its head and advised communities to make no large plans. Historic preservationists have successfully argued that the existing city should not be replaced by towers in parks, or gradually phased into a space-frame, but preserved and restored. Architects have rediscovered the virtues of architecture they had once despised as outmoded and retrograde. The energy crisis has suggested that conservation of existing structures and modest modifications to cities were more sensible than wholesale rebuilding, particularly conversion to structures as subject to energy loss as highly articulated capsules or vast controlled environments. Rapid inflation has also often made renovation better structural economics than new construction. In short, every trend of the late 1970s contradicted the premises that made the city as megastructure seem a reasonable prediction a few years earlier.

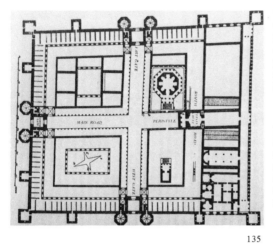

135: The emperor Diocletian, fearful of enemies both within and outside the Roman Empire, built himself a heavily fortified palace, completed early in the fourth century, on what is now the coast of Yugoslavia. The palace was large enough to function as a self-contained city; it now forms the core of the contemporary city of Spalato, or Split.

136: Elbert Peets's sketch of the royal palace of Caserta, near Naples, built in the mid-eighteenth century, shows an unfortified structure even larger than Diocletian's palace, in which all the space is given over to administrative offices and apartments for the court. The architectural organization of the palace is carried on into the landscape, making the complex appear still more like a city.

135

CASERTA

ELBERT PEETS 19

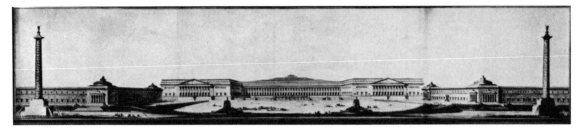

137: Given a commission in 1780 to surpass Caserta by enlarging Versailles, a proposal that seriously misjudged the political situation in France at that time, Étienne-Louis Boullée went on to design a series of projects for enormous palatial structures, 138.

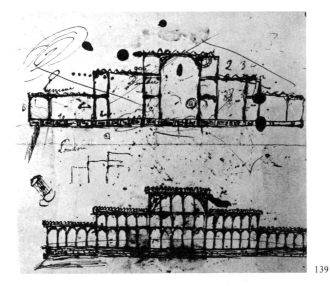

139

139, 140: *Punch* magazine named Joseph Paxton's buildings for London's 1851 Exposition the "Crystal Palace." The name, instantly accepted, recognized this unprecedented structure of iron and glass, 1,848 feet long by 408 feet wide, with a central transept 108 feet high, as belonging to the palatial tradition of buildings large enough to be self-contained cities. Paxton's original conceptual sketch shows the essential elements of the completed design.

141: Francisco Mujica added this drawing of his own to his 1929 *History of the Skyscraper.* Although not unlike Hugh Ferris's Metropolis of Tomorrow, Mujica's vision of the future stressed the interconnections among tall buildings at upper levels, a theme that had been favored by architectural illustrators since the early 1900s.

142, 143: A linear form of urban growth had been promoted by Arturo Soria y Mata starting in 1882. A modest version of Soria's idea was begun in the Madrid suburbs in 1894.

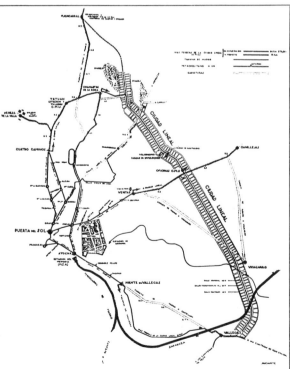

144

144, 145: Raymond Hood, like Hugh Ferris, saw the city of the future as clusters of towers in a lower urban context; his montage can be seen as an application of the Metropolis of Tomorrow to Manhattan. But Hood added another element, great bridges constructed as enormous buildings. The idea, of course, goes back to medieval times, but the technology of the modern suspension bridge permits a linear city development.

146, 147: Kenzo Tange's famous Tokyo Bay project, in which giant suspension bridges permitted the expansion of Tokyo over the water into huge, megastructural buildings.

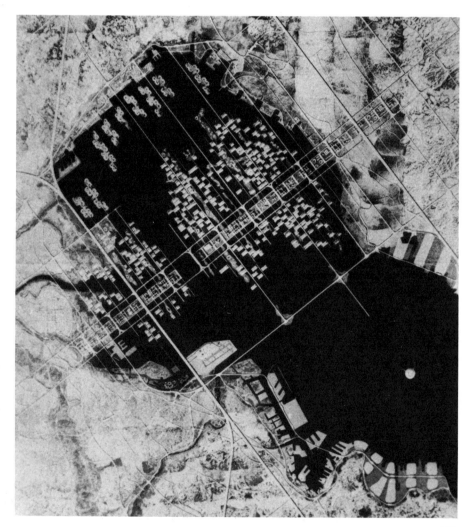

148: Paul Rudolph's Art and Architecture Building at Yale, completed in 1965, can be read as a miniature version of the kind of megastructures designed for Tokyo Bay. In this reading, each tower (in actuality only large enough to hold a small classroom or a fire stair) becomes a major office or apartment building, and the bridges between (in actuality studio spaces) become urban plazas and covered shopping centers.

148

149: That Rudolph was interested in megastructures is shown by his project for the enclosure of the Lower Manhattan Expressway and this 1967 proposal for an apartment complex to be sponsored by a graphic-art workers' trade union.

These SPACE COMIC cities reflect without conscious intention certain overtones of meaning-----illuminate an area of opinion that seeks the breakdown of conventional attitudes, the disruption of the "straight-up-and-down" formal vacuum------necessary to create a more dynamic environment.

150

150, 151, 152: Pages from *Archigram 4,* the publication of the Archigram Group of English architects, who had met at the Architectural Association School in London. Their work probably did the most to make the city as a building a popular idea within the architectural profession.

THE

ILLUSTRATION (REDRAWN) FROM 'ALPINE ARCHITECTURE BRUNO TAUT 1917-19

Most of the material on these two pages is by architects.. proving that at times they can be as wild, and as dynamic as the cartoonists. Not only this, but the schemes can all be related directly to actualities: inspiration derives from the possibilities of a material, a function or a justifiable ARCHITECTURAL gesture.
Most of the 1919-1921 material first appeared in Taut's magazine 'Frulicht'...which must have been fantastic in its originality and dynamic at the time(1920-21).
Not only this, but its validity today is realised when we compare the quality of these schemes with even the most sophisticated 'fantastic' schemes of the 1960's.

GESTURE

CATHEDRAL, CARL KRAYL 1920

'ARCHITECTURAL FORM' HANS HOLLEIN

14

'RHINE HOUSES' THEODOR GROSSE c1920

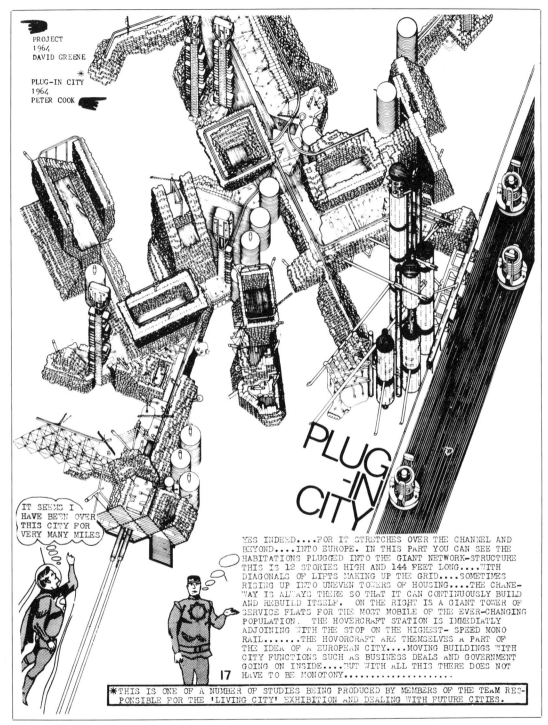

PROJECT
1964
DAVID GREENE

PLUG-IN CITY
1964
PETER COOK

PLUG
-IN
CITY

IT SEEMS I HAVE BEEN OVER THIS CITY FOR VERY MANY MILES

YES INDEED....FOR IT STRETCHES OVER THE CHANNEL AND BEYOND....INTO EUROPE. IN THIS PART YOU CAN SEE THE HABITATIONS PLUGGED INTO THE GIANT NETWORK-STRUCTURE THIS IS 12 STORIES HIGH AND 144 FEET LONG....WITH DIAGONALS OF LIFTS MAKING UP THE GRID....SOMETIMES RISING UP INTO UNEVEN TOWERS OF HOUSING....THE CRANE-WAY IS ALWAYS THERE SO THAT IT CAN CONTINUOUSLY BUILD AND REBUILD ITSELF. ON THE RIGHT IS A GIANT TOWER OF SERVICE FLATS FOR THE MOST MOBILE OF THE EVER-CHANGING POPULATION. THE HOVERCRAFT STATION IS IMMEDIATLY ADJOINING WITH THE STOP ON THE HIGHEST- SPEED MONO RAIL.......THE HOVORCRAFT ARE THEMSELVES A PART OF THE IDEA OF A EUROPEAN CITY....MOVING BUILDINGS WITH CITY FUNCTIONS SUCH AS BUSINESS DEALS AND GOVERNMENT GOING ON INSIDE....BUT WITH ALL THIS THERE DOES NOT HAVE TO BE MONOTONY....................

17

*THIS IS ONE OF A NUMBER OF STUDIES BEING PRODUCED BY MEMBERS OF THE TEaM RES- PONSIBLE FOR THE 'LIVING CITY' EXHIBITION AND DEALING WITH FUTURE CITIES.

153: Ron Herron's "Walking City Visits New York." Herron, like other members of the Archigram group, was both serious and jokey at the same time. You are being asked to believe not only that cities can be constructed to walk from one place to another but that they can walk on water as well.

154: Paolo Soleri's projects for gigantic cities are done in the name of ecological preservation, as such concentrations of people would in theory leave much of the natural landscape unencumbered. The small diagram in the corner is a profile of the Empire State Building, included by the architect to give a sense of scale.

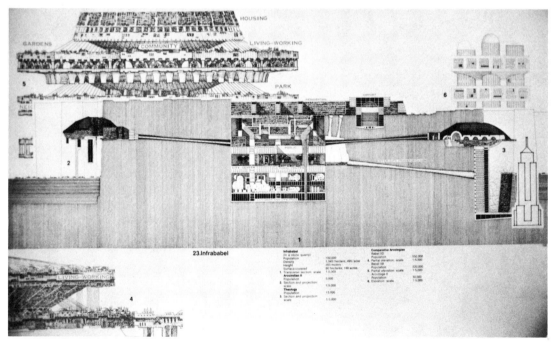

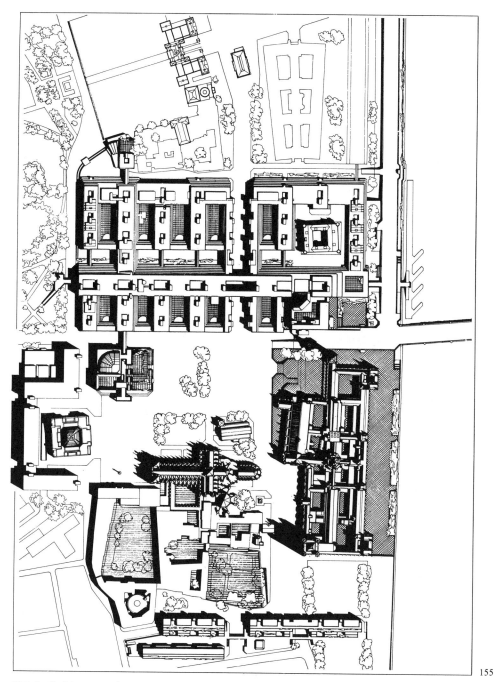

155: Leslie Martin's 1965 proposals for the precincts around the Houses of Parliament, an official government document, show how far megastructural thinking once pervaded the architectural establishment.

156, 157: Alison and Peter Smithson's Robin Hood Lane housing in the East End of London, influenced by Le Corbusier but also designed in 1963 at the height of megastructuralism, is one of many examples of how difficult it has been to translate city-as-building concepts into an attractive reality.

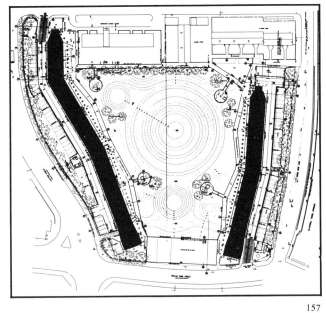

6

The Elusive City

No walls shape the city today, no pattern of railway and streetcar tracks defines corridors of growth or divides a metropolitan area into a central city surrounded by its suburbs.

Patrick Geddes observed more than seventy years ago that groups of cities were forming what he called "conurbations," so that city planning and design had become a regional problem. The urban geographer Jean Gottmann wrote his famous *Megalopolis* study in 1961. Megalopolis was the name Gottmann gave to the continuous strip of urbanized area that stretches from Washington, D.C., to Boston, Massachusetts, and which today would probably be defined as stretching from Richmond, Virginia, to Portland, Maine. The definition of a megalopolis has since been applied to other urbanized corridors, such as the Randstad in the Netherlands; Tokaido, which includes the cities of Tokyo, Yokohama, Osaka, Nagoya and Kobe; or the whole of the upper midwestern United States from Pittsburgh to Chicago.

Rural areas within a megalopolis are not what they seem to be. For example, in a state like Connecticut almost every resident makes a living from nonfarm employment, despite extensive tracts of open country; and woodland grows back over what were once fields and pastures. Rural areas outside a megalopolis are often not what they seem to be, either. The presence of a sophisticated French restaurant or a designer clothing boutique often shows that a seemingly pastoral village is really a summer or winter vacation colony for city people.

Over three quarters of the people in the United States live in areas that urban geographers would classify as urban, and proportions are similar or greater in other technologically advanced countries.

Even in agricultural areas today's well-traveled farmer-executive operating a computer and complex farm machinery is hardly a country bumpkin. The whole idea of provincialism is difficult to maintain when an entire population watches the same television programs and reads the same national newsmagazines and newspapers.

The jet airplane has also made it possible for a professor at M.I.T. to commute to a consultancy with an electronics firm in Houston, or for an international banker or lawyer based in New York to spend a week out of every month in Tokyo or London. Parisian families live all summer in East Hampton, New York; New York families spend the summer in Spain. As a result, it not only becomes more and more difficult to distinguish between rural and urban areas; it is no longer as clear where one city's influence ends and another's begins.

And what is a city? It has become commonplace for people who live in big metropolitan areas to say: "I never go downtown anymore." They can work in a modern office building or factory, shop at the best department stores and boutiques, attend theaters and concerts, see first-run movies and eat in excellent restaurants, all without ever setting foot in areas legally defined as cities.

In these respects Ebenezer Howard's idea of a new kind of urban life that combined the advantages of city and country has been realized, partly through government policies (particularly in Europe) and partly through unguided interaction of economic and social forces. What are missing are the benefits of design: the greenbelts and orderly clusters of development that Howard imagined. Howard also expected the old cities to wither away. In this he was at least partly wrong; downtowns are feeling competitive pressures never known before, but are responding by assuming new specialized functions.

Downtowns in the big metropolitan centers today are for big office buildings, conventions, tourists and, in a few of the largest cities, the homes of the rich and some young professionals. Certain kinds of business, like banks and corporate headquarters, still need large staffs of clerical workers and benefit from a central location with good public transportation. The skyline includes both office towers and hotels, the hotels supported by a convention center, a "festival market place" and restored historic districts. The old city's cultural life is also still strong: its museums, theaters and universities.

The downtown department stores, if they are still there, serve a new mix of office workers, tourists and residents of the close-in city neighborhoods. If fashionable shopping remains in the city center, it is likely to be in a midtown area near the hotels and the expensive downtown residential districts.

Outside the still vibrant downtowns of the big metropolitan areas, much of the older city continues on a downward curve. The railway tracks are lined by empty factory buildings; neighborhoods are decayed and even abandoned; public housing projects are often in disrepair. While some older neighborhoods on the fashionable side of town are still in good condition or are being "gentrified," they are only a small part of the picture.

The real centers of urban life have moved to what were once fashionable suburbs. What had been small suburban downtowns are now office centers; the regional shopping malls often have more and better stores than downtown, restaurants and theaters have sprung up along shopping strips that used to offer only filling stations and supermarkets. Corporate offices nestle in old estates or are grouped in office parks.

The airport and the road leading to it has created a new urban center, with offices, factories and warehouses, and clusters of hotels.

Beyond the old fashionable suburbs, but still on the preferred side of the city, an entirely new urban world has sprung up in the past ten or twenty years. It has no center but is roughly fan-shaped, with a highway or main arterial road serving as an extended main street. Here office parks, motels and shopping malls alternate with garden apartment developments and closely grouped houses. These are not the sprawling suburban streets created a generation ago, but tightly organized colonies, often with a fence and gatehouse.

Factories and warehouses may also be found in this district, although most have migrated to less expensive suburban locations, where they are grouped in industrial parks and spread out along highways. Factory workers may commute outward from older suburban and urban neighborhoods, or live in tract housing or mobile homes in what were, until a few years ago, small rural communities.

This pattern, expressed in new construction in many parts of the United States, can also be found in older, more settled areas like the districts west and southwest of London, where older cities and towns are assuming new functions as office and research centers, and drawing a new type of resident as a consequence.

There are, of course, still cities and towns that are not part of a larger metropolitan structure, but there is almost no city that is not part of a national influence system of newsmagazines and television programs, credit cards, chain stores, franchised fast food and hotels, and major travel networks. In these smaller cities, forces of decentralization and reconstruction of the old downtown are at work in ways analogous to those shaping the great metropolis. The downtown shopping is likely to have migrated to a suburban center, and the suburban shopping strip of franchised food and service stations probably does more business than downtown, although the old center may well be fighting back with new trees and sidewalk paving along the main shopping street. Local corporate headquarters and factories are often located away from downtown. Houses in some old neighborhoods are being restored, but almost everyone in a small city who can afford it seems to prefer a house set in lawns and gardens to more urban ways of life, and smaller cities, too, are spreading across the landscape. Nor are small cities free of the poverty and neglect, closed factories and deteriorated housing that are found in the metropolis.

Modern cities large and small show the influences of all the major city-design ideas. Monumental design has given form to groups of civic and cultural buildings, created public parks and boulevards, and provided a heritage of actual monuments: columns, obelisks, even triumphal arches. Monumental building groupings are also to be found on the older part of the local university campus. The garden city and garden suburb have shaped the fashionable residential districts and, in a more diluted form, the newer suburban subdivisions. Modernist ideas of city organization have helped create public housing projects and downtown urban renewal districts, as well as the design of tall office buildings, office parks and hospital complexes. The concept of the city as a megastructure may well be reflected in the design of regional shopping centers and airports, and in a downtown business district where office buildings, hotels and shops are connected by interior atria and networks of pedestrian bridges or tunnels.

As we have seen, each of these city-design concepts in its day was put forward as a comprehensive solution to give form to a whole urban area, and each turned out to be a great deal less effective than its proponents had hoped.

The monumental city, as advocated by Daniel Burnham and Edward Bennett in the 1909 plan for Chicago, was unable to provide a mechanism for shaping groups of tall buildings and controlling the unevenness of development that characterized private real-estate investment.

The garden suburb was a reaction to the city as it had evolved during the nineteenth century. It was not originally intended as a substitute for the city but depended upon the existence of a central business district. It was Ebenezer Howard who turned the garden suburb into a comprehensive city-design concept by postulating a self-sufficient garden city instead of a suburb, with the old metropolis replaced by additional clusters of garden cities. The way urban areas have spread through the use of automobiles has made it almost impossible to limit the size and extent of garden cities in the way that Howard had imagined during the railroad age; and the decentralization of urban functions has diluted the old relationships between suburbs and city center. The result is the familiar transportation problem of today's suburbanized metropolis: everything is a long drive from everything else.

The concept of a modern city was also a reaction against the way cities had evolved during the nineteenth century. The old forms of urban organization provided by street and square were discarded in favor of the individual building in a parklike setting. Implicit in this design idea was the belief that cities would be completely renewed, except for a few structures retained for historical or sentimental reasons. There was thus to be no incongruity between new buildings and old. There was also an expectation that modern architecture would replace the diversity of styles that had characterized nineteenth- and early-twentieth-century buildings with a single, unified architectural expression, and that this stylistic unity would be conferred on cities. Neither expectation was justified: most cities, even those badly damaged by bombs, could not be completely renewed, and modernism did not bring stylistic unity. Although older buildings constructed on street frontages often received deficient amounts of light and air, the street turned out to be the primary mechanism of human interaction in cities. When it was eliminated, no amount of park or plaza could take its place. The fragments of cities that have been rebuilt as collections of buildings set in public open space, or the new communi-

ties designed on similar principles, have seldom been perceived as satis-
factory environments.

Theorists of the city as megastructure thought that they had an answer to the fragmentation and disunity of modern architecture: the city
would become a continuous building, and instead of either a street or a
plaza there would be a controlled interior environment. This concept,
however, went against the ways in which city development was normally
financed, and by requiring total reconstruction of the city, it also went
against the increasingly strong public and political support for historic
preservation, for community participation and for energy efficiency and
conservation of the natural environment. While megastructural city-
design ideas had an important effect on architecture, and are still influenc-
ing what is built in cities, the megastructure as a comprehensive theory
of city design has few advocates today.

By contrast, monumental city design, not long ago discarded as an
irrelevant and outmoded set of ideas, has been gaining new interest. Leon
Krier, who in the late 1960s was working for James Stirling on a megastructural design for the Siemens headquarters project in Munich, began
his monumental planning concepts as a reaction to the megastructure, but
also in evolution from it. Straight lines of communication typical of
megastructure design became a monumental axis. This transition is clearly
visible in Krier's Leinfelden City Center project of 1971, where the main
and cross axes are lined with continuous, large-scale buildings, and the
intersection of the two axes is the site for a cluster of what looks like four
identical modern office buildings. Krier in his more recent projects reso-
lutely refuses to deal definitively either with groups of tall buildings or
with automobiles, which end up being excluded from his monumental-
city concepts.

Low-rise high-density housing is a design problem that has increased
in importance to architects as they have tried to devise modern buildings
that will fit into more traditional urban relationships. The housing designed by Josef Kliehues for the Wedding district in Berlin in 1978, in
which five-story buildings follow the streetline around the perimeter of
the block and form a courtyard, is precisely the building type that was
abandoned by modernist German architects in the 1920s in favor of
parallel rows of housing sited for most favorable exposure to sunlight.

The ideas that spaces should be enclosed and given definitive form, and that there should be design continuity from building to building, are aspects of the monumental-city design tradition that are being given more and more attention. The planners of many university campuses are now trying to restore these traditional spatial relationships, which are usually implicit in the original plan, but were abandoned during the 1950s and 1960s. Because of the tall building and the incremental, block-by-block development of cities, it is hard to recreate monumental spatial relationships in the city center. However, architects are now siting buildings to terminate axes, and giving towers a monumental base, where it helps to fit the new building into the existing urban context. The zoning ordinances of cities, including New York, Pittsburgh and San Francisco, are being amended to encourage design continuity, the preservation of street walls, plazas as clearly defined space, and other traditional aspects of city design that were legislated away by tower-in-park ordinances of the 1960s.

A revival of interest in the picturesque principles that lay behind garden-city and garden-suburb design is also in progress. Raymond Unwin's 1909 *Town Planning in Practice,* with its sympathetic treatment of Camillo Sitte's city-design ideas, is being read again, as is Sitte himself. Christopher Alexander and his associate authors of the books *The Timeless Way of Building* and *A Pattern Language,* which were published in the late 1970s, have adopted the methodology of Camillo Sitte in looking at places that had been perfected over a long period of time in preindustrial societies, deducing design principles from them, and then advocating these principles as applicable to new construction.

Recent thinking about tall buildings in urban areas is that they should be contained within a matrix of pedestrian-oriented uses and that public spaces when they occur should be designed to attract use, not simply to provide a setting for buildings. There is increasing suspicion about residential tall buildings for any group other than the rich, who can afford the staff necessary to make such structures secure, and a vacation house somewhere closer to the ground. The tower in the park, however, retains the powerful image that was created by Le Corbusier, the C.I.A.M. and the advocates of modernism in architecture. Generations of architects have been trained to design in this way; and the public has been educated to accept the tower in a parklike setting as an inevitable accompaniment of modern life. In many cities, particularly in countries that are just now entering the industrial age, the tall tower continues to play the role that Le Corbusier devised for it in his 1930 Algiers plan: artillery shells destroying the fabric of the older city.

While Reyner Banham wrote of the megastructure as "urban futures of the recent past," it has proved possible to give megastructural ideas a practicality that eluded some of their original designers. The downtown business district of the city of Minneapolis has been gradually turning into a megastructure through the construction of a network of pedestrian bridges that link new and existing buildings. The nearby city of St. Paul has been following a similar policy, and the downtown shopping district in Milwaukee has recently been rebuilt to make it into a linear enclosed environment linked by bridges. Underground pedestrian concourse systems in Montreal, Osaka and Houston perform a similar function, but without the drama created by the glassed-in pedestrian walkway spanning streets.

The center-city atrium, too, is becoming a commonplace of city design. Often several buildings look into the atrium space, which is also an urban shopping center. Escalators cut diagonally through the space, and elevators are dramatized as glass capsules. The association of atrium and glass elevator was first made by John Portman in his design for a hotel in Atlanta completed in 1967, at the height of the excitement about megastructure design.

The technology of automated rapid transit has also improved to the point that it is now possible to build some of the ideas imagined by megastructuralists decades ago. Perimeter parking garages connected by automated rapid transit to city centers are now much closer to being economically feasible, and may, in turn, assist in the reinstatement of some monumental-design concepts by removing parking as a center-city land use.

The city has become so vast and encompasses so many different densities of development, so many different kinds of activity and such a variety of communities that it is unlikely that any single design concept could emerge to give form to a metropolitan area in the way that Renaissance theorists might draw an idealized Vitruvian city as a polygonal street plan surrounded by ramparts. In the same way, modern architecture includes such a diversity of building types and construction methods and western society permits such latitude of individual expression that it is unlikely that a single new architectural style will emerge comparable to the uniform architectural expression observable in preindustrial societies, with strong social hierarchies, and little knowledge of how things were done in other places.

Attempts to reshape the city to a static pattern failed even during the Renaissance, as economic and social change were too rapid and too complicated to be contained. How much more difficult it would be to accomplish the same task today. What is needed now is not a new all-purpose city-design concept, but new ways of integrating city design with the process of economic and social change. Then, and only then, will the design of our cities live up to the promise to be found in a few special neighborhoods, and in the best individual buildings.

Bibliographical Notes

Chapter 1: Preindustrial Traditions

For summaries of the urban geographer's current understanding of preindustrial cities, see Chapter 7 of D. I. Scargill's *The Form of Cities* (London: Bell & Hyman, 1979) and Part I of Harold Carter's *An Introduction to Urban Historical Geography* (London: Edward Arnold, 1983). The best general treatment of the preindustrial city in relation to the development of western culture and technology remains that to be found in Lewis Mumford's *The City in History* (New York: Harcourt Brace, 1961). R. E. Wycherley's *How the Greeks Built Cities* (New York: Macmillan, 1962) gives an excellent description of a city type that is still deeply embedded in western cultural traditions. See also Joseph Rykwert's *The Idea of a Town: The Anthropology of Urban Form in Rome, Italy, and the Ancient World* (Princeton, N.J.: Princeton University Press, 1976).

The *Ten Books on Architecture* by Vitruvius can be read in Morris Hickey Morgan's translation, reprinted by Dover in 1960 from the Harvard University Press edition of 1914. For Vitruvius's influence on Renaissance ideal cities, see Part 1 of *The Ideal City* by Helen Rosenau (London: Routledge and Kegan Paul, 1959); for the effect of fortifications on cities, see *Military Considerations in City Planning* by Horst de La Croix (New York: Braziller, 1972).

Chapter 2: The Monumental City

T. F. Reddaway's *The Rebuilding of London* (London: Jonathan Cape, 1940) is still a definitive account. Reddaway, however, was so anxious to prove that Wren's plan was not rejected without consideration that he tends to undervalue the plan itself. *Wren's London,* by Eric de Maré (London: The Folio Society, 1975), is a well-illustrated account of the Great Fire and its aftermath. Karl Gruber's *Ein Deutsche Stadt* (Munich: Bruckmann, 1914) uses the development of a fictional city to illustrate what was happening almost everywhere, and thus provides a means of comparison between London and other cities of its time. There are monographs on Wren by, among others, John Summerson, Kerry Downes and Bryan Little. Memoirs of the Wren family were published in 1750 by Stephen Wren under the title *Parentalia.*

Sigfried Giedion's *Space, Time and Architecture,* originally published by the Harvard University Press in 1941, while partisan in its account of modern architecture, contains a brilliantly compressed description of the relationship between perspective and urban planning and of the origins of Sixtus V's Rome. Both chapters were added to the third edition, which first appeared in 1954. Chapter 5 of Jacob Bronowsky's *The Ascent of Man* (Boston: Little Brown, 1973) also describes the relationship between Renaissance science and art, particularly the influence of perspective on painting.

As noted in the text, John Summerson's research plays an important role in understanding the work of Inigo Jones, John Wood senior and junior, and John Nash in the development of city design. Summerson's *Inigo Jones* (London: Penguin Books, 1966) is a more extended treatment of material that was included in his *Georgian London,* originally published in 1945, and brought out by Pelican Books in a revised edition in 1962. "John Wood and the English Town-Planning Tradition" appears in John Summerson's *Heavenly Mansions* (London: Cresset Press, 1949). Nash is discussed in *Georgian London* and in Summerson's *Architecture in Britain 1530–1830* (London: Penguin Books, 1953). Summerson, unlike many art historians, writes beautifully and conveys a sense of how things really happened.

The urban square as a building type is the subject of Paul Zucker's *Town and Square* (New York: Columbia University Press, 1959).

"The Genealogy of L'Enfant's Washington," by Elbert Peets, appeared serially in the *Journal of the American Institute of Architects,* April, May and June 1927. L'Enfant's correspondence while working on the plan for Washington was edited by Elizabeth S. Kite and published by the Johns Hopkins Press (Baltimore, MD) in 1929 under the title *L'Enfant and Washington.* Anyone who has ever worked on a large planning project will find much that is familiar as the sequence of letters unfolds.

Understanding the difference between the way monumental city-design concepts were used during the Renaissance and in the modern period requires a knowledge of the changes that took place in architectural theory. Joseph Rykwert's *The First Moderns* (Cambridge, MA: M.I.T. Press, 1980) seeks to trace the development of a new architectural sensibility through close reading of

theoretical texts published in the seventeenth and eighteenth centuries. Rykwert's former pupil Alberto Perez-Gomez uses a parallel method in his *Architecture and the Crisis of Modern Science,* which relates changes in architectural theory from a system of beliefs to an experimental and pragmatic attitude to parallel changes taking place in scientific methods. See also "Durand and the Continuity of Tradition," by Werner Szambien, in *The Beaux Arts,* edited by Robin Middleton (London: Thames and Hudson, 1982).

A. Trystan Edward's appreciation of John Nash's Regent Street appears in *Good and Bad Manners in Architecture* (London: Philip Alan, 1924). There is a well-illustrated description of Nash's Regent Street in Edmund Bacon's *Design of Cities* (New York: Penguin Books, 1976).

Sigfried Giedion's *Space, Time and Architecture,* cited above, contains a good account of Haussmann's rebuilding of Paris. *Les Promenades de Paris,* by Haussmann's collaborator, the landscape architect Jean Alphand, was reissued by the Princeton Architectural Press (Princeton, NJ) in 1985. For Robert Moses on Haussmann, see the *Architectural Forum,* July 1942, "What Happened to Haussmann?"

Camillo Sitte's *Der Stadte-Bau nach seinen kunstersichen Grundsatzen,* originally published in Vienna in 1889, was translated by George R. Collins and Christiane C. Collins and published by Random House (New York) in 1965 under the title *City Planning According to Artistic Principles.* See also the same authors' *Camillo Sitte and the Birth of Modern City Planning* (New York: Random House, 1965).

The biography of Daniel Burnham by Charles Moore, first published in 1921, has been reprinted by the Da Capo Press (New York, 1966). In 1970 Da Capo also reprinted the 1909 *Plan for Chicago,* by Daniel Burnham and Edward H. Bennett. These two books together give a clear picture of

Burnham's development as a city designer. See also "Toward an 'Imperial City': Daniel H. Burnham and the City Beautiful Movement," by Mario Manieri-Elia, translated by Barbara Luigia La Penta, in *The American City from the Civil War to the New Deal* (Cambridge, MA: M.I.T. Press, 1979).

For Canberra, see Walter Burley Griffin, *The Federal City,* and James Birrell's monograph *Walter Burley Griffin,* 1964. *Indian Summer: Lutyens, Baker and Imperial Delhi,* by Robert Grant Irving (New Haven, CT: Yale University Press, 1981), is an extensive and well-illustrated account of the design and construction of the new capital. For a viewpoint that is less sympathetic to the British, see also the chapter on New Delhi in Sten Nilsson's *The New Capitals of India, Pakistan and Bangladesh,* translated by Elisabeth Andreasson (Scandinavian Institute for Asian Studies, 1973).

An "Interview with Albert Speer," by Francesco Dal Co and Sergio Polano, appeared in *Oppositions* 12 (Spring 1978). The same issue contains Kenneth Frampton's "A Synoptic View of the Architecture of the Third Reich."

As noted in the text, "Collage City," by Colin Rowe and Fred Koetter, in the *Architectural Review* of August 1975, was followed by the book *Collage City,* by the same authors, published by the M.I.T. Press (Cambridge, MA) in 1978. Somewhere in the transition from article to book a great deal of clarity was lost.

For Roma Interrotta, see "Roma Interrotta," edited by Michael Graves, in *Architectural Design* 49 (March 1979).

Leon Krier, Houses, Palaces, Cities, edited by Demetri Porphyrios (London: Architectural Design Editions, 1984), is the most complete monograph on Leon Krier. Rob Krier's *Urban Space,* translated by Christine Czechowski and George Black, was published by Rizzoli (New York) in 1979. See also *Rob Krier, Urban Projects 1968–1982* (New York: Rizzoli for the Institute for Ar-chitecture and Urban Studies, 1982).

The Museum of Modern Art (New York) published an exhibition catalogue in 1985: *Ricardo Bofill and Leon Krier, Architecture Urbanism and History.*

The Harvard Architecture Review 4 (Spring 1984) was devoted to the subject "Monumentality and The City," including the proceedings of a forum held at Harvard in December 1981. It provides an insight into the adjustments being made to architectural theory as a result of the re-emergence in practice of monumental city-design concepts and more historical reminiscence in buildings. See in particular Christiane C. and George R. Collins's historical survey of references to monumentality in the literature of modern architecture, "Monumentality: A Critical Matter in Modern Architecture."

Chapter 3: The Garden City

Ebenezer Howard's *Garden Cities of To-morrow* is available in an edition, first published by Faber and Faber (London) in 1945, that restores portions of the original text edited out after the first edition. The work of restoration was done by Frederick J. Osborne, who also contributed a preface, and there is an introductory essay by Lewis Mumford. *Sir Ebenezer Howard and the Town Planning Movement* is a rather quaintly written memoir by Dugald MacFayden that includes biographical statements by Howard and members of his family. Originally published in 1933 by the University of Manchester Press, it was reprinted in 1970. *The Building of Satellite Towns,* by C. B. Purdom, originally published by J. M. Dent (London) in 1925 and revised and republished in 1949, contains the most complete documentation of the development of Letchworth and Welwyn, presented as a sophisticated how-to book. The revised edition appeared just as Howard's New Towns corporations were being taken over by the British government. An excellent modern monograph on Howard is the section entitled "Ebenezer Howard" of Robert Fishman's *Urban Utopias in the Twentieth Century* (New York: Basic Books, 1977).

For a more general discussion of model company towns, garden suburbs and garden cities, see Walter L. Creese, *The Search for Environment* (New Haven, CT: Yale University Press, 1966). Leonardo Benevolo's *The Origins of Modern Town Planning,* translated by Judith Landry (Cambridge, MA: M.I.T. Press, 1971), puts much of its emphasis on nineteenth-century social reform and utopian proposals. See also Lewis Mumford's *The Story of Utopias,* originally published in 1922, as a good accompaniment to a study of Howard.

On Raymond Unwin and Barry Parker, see Raymond Unwin's *Town Planning in Practice* (London: Unwin, 1909); also Walter L. Creese, *The Legacy of Raymond Unwin* (Cambridge, MA: Harvard University Press, 1977).

The Picturesque: Studies in a Point of View, by Christopher Hussey, who was for many years the editor of *Country Life,* was from the time of its publication in 1927 until recently the best introduction to the subject short of reading Sir Uvedale Price or Richard Payne Knight. The British periodical *The Architectural Review* campaigned for picturesque design principles after World War II, including the *Townscape* drawings of Gordon Cullen, who at one time was a member of the *Review's* editorial staff. However, it remained for David Watkin to bring the full force of modern art-historical scholarship to bear on *The English Vision: The Picturesque in Architecture, Landscape and Garden Design* (New York: Icon Editions, Harper & Row,

1982), a comprehensive, and well-written study. For the Queen Anne style, see Mark Girouard's *Sweetness and Light, The Queen Anne Movement 1860–1900* (New Haven, CT: Yale University Press, 1977) and Andrew Saint's *Richard Norman Shaw* (Yale, 1976).

"A Patriarchal Utopia: The Garden City and Housing Reform in Germany at the Turn of the Century," by Franziska Bollerey and Kristiana Hartmann, is included in *The Rise of Modern Urban Planning 1800–1914,* edited by Anthony Sutcliffe (New York: St. Martin's, 1980). Other useful sources for German garden housing or model company towns include *Neue Baukunst in Den Rheinlanden,* by Richard Klapheck (Dusseldorf, c. 1928), and Walter Muller-Wulckow, *Wohnbauten und Seidlungen* (Langewiesche, 1929).

"The Anglo-American Suburb," edited by Robert A. M. Stern with John Montague Massengale, in *Architectural Design* 51 (October–November 1981), is a useful and interesting compilation. For good accounts of U.S. housing during World War I from different perspectives, see Mel Scott's *American City Planning Since 1890* (Berkeley: University of California Press, 1969) and the parallel account in *A Concise History of American Architecture,* by Leland M. Roth (New York: Icon Editions, Harper & Row, 1979). Many of the World War I housing designs were published in *The Housing Book,* by William P. Comstock (New York: Comstock, 1919).

London Housing, published by the London County Council in 1937, shows cottage estates and other subsidized housing built by the County Council and individual borough councils up to that date.

Clarence Stein is the best source on his own work and also includes a history of the greenbelt towns in his *Towards New Towns for America,* published originally in 1951, available in paperback from the M.I.T. Press (Cambridge, MA). There is an introduction by Lewis Mumford that calls the work described in the book "but finger exercises, preparing for symphonies that are yet to come." Volume 7 of the *The Regional Survey of New York and Its Environs, Neighborhood and Community Planning* contains Clarence Perry's monograph "The Neighborhood Unit," as well as "The Problems of Planning Unbuilt Areas," by Thomas Adams, Edward M. Bassett and Robert Whitten; this volume was published as part of the New York Regional Plan in 1929.

A good account of U.S. housing policies between the wars can be found in *The Urban Pattern: City Planning and Design,* by Arthur B. Gallion and Simon Eisner (New York: Van Nostrand Reinhold 1950), and subsequent editions.

There is, of course, an enormous literature dealing with the work of Frank Lloyd Wright, and Wright was a prolific author himself. For the final version of Wright's ideas about cities, see his *The Living City* (New York: Horizon Press, 1958), which incorporates portions of *The Disappearing City* (1932) and *When Democracy Builds* (1945). See also Giorgio Ciucci, "The City in Agrarian Ideology and Frank Lloyd Wright," in *The American City,* cited above, and the section on Wright in Robert Fishman's *Urban Utopias in the Twentieth Century,* also cited previously.

For an excellent description of new-towns policy in Great Britain and France see *Urban and Regional Planning,* by Peter Hall (New York: John Wiley, Halsted Press, 1975). *New Towns in America,* compiled by the American Institute of Architects and edited by James Bailey (New York: John Wiley, 1973), is an index of the comparable U.S. experience.

Chapter 4: The Modern City

H. Heathcote Statham's *Modern Architecture* (London: Chapman and Hall, 1897) provides an interesting insight into turn-of-the-century architectural politics in England. Carl Schorske's *Fin de Siècle Vienna,* 1980, contains a comparable account of cultural issues in Austria, from which is drawn the quotation from Otto Wagner given in the text.

The most accessible source on Garnier is *Tony Garnier: The Cité Industrielle,* by Dora Wiebenson (New York: Braziller, 1969).

For Berlage, see P. Singelenberg, *H. P. Berlage: Idea and Style, the Quest for Modern Architecture,* 1972, also *Dr. H. P. Berlage En Zijn Werk,* by K. P. C. De Bazel and other authors (Rotterdam, 1916), which has some good illustrations of Berlage's city plans. *The Amsterdam School: Dutch Expressionist Architecture, 1915–1930,* edited by Wim de Wit and published by the M.I.T. Press (Cambridge, MA) in 1983, has an extended treatment of architecture and social context but little about the plans the buildings were carrying out.

The literature by and about Le Corbusier is so large as to constitute almost a subject in itself. The principal source book, however, is the 7-volume *Oeuvre Complete,* edited by Willy Boesiger and published by Les Editions d'Architecture (Zurich). Most readers of English have been introduced to Le Corbusier's thought through Frederick Etchell's 1927 translation, *Towards a New Architecture,* of Le Corbusier's 1923 *Vers une Architecture. Concerning Town Planning* (London: Architectural Press, 1947) was translated by Clive Entwistle from Le Corbusier's *Propos D'Urbanisme,* published in Paris the previous year. Le Corbusier's *When the Cathedrals Were White,* translated by Francis E. Hyslop and published in the United States in 1947, is a good summary of Le Corbusier's developed opinions about city design. Robert Fishman's segment on

Le Corbusier in *Urban Utopias of the Twentieth Century,* cited previously, is particularly good on Le Corbusier's politics.

Ernst May, passed over almost completely in so many histories of modern architecture, is discussed in Hans-Reiner Müller-Raemisch's "Stadtplanung in Frankfurt am Main," and individual projects by May are described by Heinz Ulrich Krauss, both in *Bauen in Frankfurt am Main seit 1900* (Frankfurt, 1977). See also references to May in *Modern Architecture,* by Bruno Taut (London: The Studio, 1929), and in Gallion and Eisner's *The Urban Pattern,* cited earlier, and Kenneth Frampton's brief but knowing comments in his *Modern Architecture: A Critical History* (Oxford, 1980).

On European housing between the wars, see Catherine Bauer's *Modern Housing* (Boston: Houghton Mifflin, 1934) and accounts by Taut and Gallion and Eisner, cited above. See also Roger Sherwood's *Modern Housing Prototypes* (Cambridge, MA: Harvard University Press, 1978).

A history of the early years of C.I.A.M. can be found in Sigfried Giedion's introduction to *Can Our Cities Survive?,* edited by José Sert (Cambridge, MA: Harvard University Press, 1941). The story of C.I.A.M. continues in *A Decade of New Architecture,* edited by Sigfried Giedion (Zurich: Editions Girsberger, 1951). See also Reyner Banham's entry on C.I.A.M. in *Encyclopedia of Modern Architecture,* edited by Gerd Hatje, United States edition (New York: Harry N. Abrams, 1964).

Modern Architecture, International Exhibition, the catalogue published by the Museum of Modern Art (New York) makes an interesting comparison to the more ideological *The International Style,* by Henry Russell Hitchcock and Philip Johnson, also 1932 and published in conjunction with the same exhibition. *The International Style* was republished by Norton with Hitchcock's 1951 *Architectural Record* article, "The International Style Twenty Years Later," in which Hitch-

cock ate some of his earlier words.

The Metropolis of Tomorrow, by Hugh Ferris, originally published in 1929 by Ives Washburn, has been reissued by the Princeton Architectural Press (Princeton, NJ) in 1985.

The most widely read books about modern architecture, in addition to Giedion's *Space, Time and Architecture,* cited previously, have been Nikolaus Pevsner's *Pioneers of the Modern Movement,* originally published in 1936 and prudently retitled *Pioneers of Modern Design* in editions published after 1960, and J. M. Richards, *Introduction to Modern Architecture,* first published in 1940. These three books helped create a new kind of architectural history in which much of what was actually happening during the modern period was excluded because it shouldn't have been happening as far as the authors of these histories were concerned. Giedion had a strong interest in city design, although his ideological commitments caused him to leave out important figures like Ernst May and Clarence Stein; but it is remarkable how little Pevsner and Richards had to say about modernist concepts of city design, and how little attention has been given to city design by other historians and theorists whose view of modern architecture had been cast in a similar mold.

Vincent Scully has been a pioneer in enlarging concepts of modernism in architecture to include the design of cities. His *Modern Architecture* (New York: Braziller, 1961, revised 1974) and *American Architecture and Urbanism* (New York: Praeger, 1969) have other virtues, but are important for including urban design issues. See also Scully's "The Death of the Street," in *Perspecta 8* (New Haven, 1963). Kenneth Frampton's *Modern Architecture,* cited above, also deals with urbanistic issues, although still within the critical framework that Giedion, Pevsner and Richards helped create. For another revisionist view of modern architecture, see the introduction by Colin

Row to *Five Architects: Eisenman, Graves, Gwathmey, Hejduk, Meier* (New York: Wittenborn, 1972; reprinted by Oxford University Press, 1975).

The definitive critique of the effect of modern architecture on cities is still Jane Jacobs' *The Death and Life of Great American Cities* (New York, 1961). See also *Cities in a Race with Time,* by Jeanne R. Lowe (New York: Random House, 1967), for well-researched descriptions of the urban-renewal process in major American cities.

Kell Åström's *City Planning in Sweden,* translated by Rudy Feichtner for the Swedish Institute for Cultural Relations with Foreign Countries, 1967, is a revised edition of a book originally published in Sweden under the title *Svensk stadsplanering.* It is a useful summary. Good capsule descriptions of Vallingby and Farsta can be found in *Planning for Man and Motor,* by Paul Ritter (New York: Macmillan, 1964). *Rebuilding Cities,* by Percy Johnson Marshall (Hawthorne, NY: Aldine, 1966), contains a lengthy description of the postwar reconstruction of London, in which Johnson-Marshall played an executive role. There is also a good chapter on the reconstruction of Rotterdam.

Victor Gruen's *Centers for the Urban Environment* (New York: Van Nostrand Reinhold, 1973) includes a description of the genesis of his Fort Worth plan.

Maxwell Fry's recollections about the design of Chandigarh can be found in *The Open Hand: Essays on Le Corbusier,* edited by Russell Walden (Cambridge, MA: M.I.T. Press, 1977).

Norma Evenson's *Paris: A Century of Change, 1878–1978* (New Haven, CT: Yale University Press, 1979) has good accounts of modern French urban renewal, city improvements, housing and new-towns policies, all described in relation to the historical fabric of Paris and particularly the work of Haussmann.

Robert Venturi, Denise Scott Brown and Steven Izenouer have written far more about architectural symbolism than city design in their *Learning from Las Vegas,* most easily read in the 1977 revised edition, published by M.I.T. Press. However, this book contains many interesting observations about the nature of the modern city, and is one of the few theoretical works that seek to relate architecture and city design to what is actually happening to the development of the modern metropolis.

Chapter 5: Megastructures: The City as a Building

A good descriptive compilation of modern city development in the United States can be found in the *Comparative Metropolitan Analysis Project,* conducted under the editorship of John S. Adams. There is a *Comparative Atlas of America's Great Cities* (Minneapolis: University of Minnesota Press, 1976) and twenty geographical vignettes of American cities, published as *Contemporary Metropolitan America* (Cambridge, MA: Ballinger, 1976). *Megalopolis,* by Jean Gottmann, originally published in 1961, is a classic description of the organization of the modern metropolis. It is available in an M.I.T. Press paperback. See also "Megalopolitan Systems Around the World," by Jean Gottmann, in *Ekistics* 243 (February 1976), and Homer Hoyt, "Recent Distortions of the Classical Models of Urban Structure," in *Land Economics* 40 (May 1964).

The reference in the text to George Hersey is to his *Architecture, Poetry and Number in the Royal Palace at Caserta* (New Haven, CT: Yale University Press, 1983).

Françoise Choay's *The Modern City: Planning in the 19th Century* (New York:

Braziller, 1969) contains a number of interesting illustrations relevant to this chapter, including Henry-Jules Borie's Aerodomes. See also G. F. Chadwick, *The World of Sir Joseph Paxton,* 1961. Leonardo Benevolo, in *The Origins of Modern Town Planning,* cited above, is particularly useful on nineteenth-century utopias and the influence of Fourier. See also *The Architecture of Fantasy: Utopian Building and Planning in Modern Times,* by Ulrich Conrads and Hans G. Sperlich, translated, edited and expanded by Christiane C. Collins and George R. Collins (New York: Praeger, 1962), *Yesterday's Tomorrows*, by Joseph J. Corn and Brian Horrigan (New York: Summit Books, 1984). and the chapter on Bruno Taut and Glasarchitektur in Dennis Sharp's *Modern Architecture and Expressionism* (New York: Braziller, 1966).

For Buckminster Fuller, see *The Dymaxion World of Buckminster Fuller,* by Robert Marks (New York: Reinhold, 1960).

One account of the Metabolist movement is Kisho Kurokawa's *Metabolism in Architecture* (Boulder, CO: Westview Press, 1977). See also *Beyond Metabolism: The New Japanese Architecture,* by Michael Franklin (New York: Architectural Record Books, 1978). The collected works of *Archigram,* edited by Peter Cook, were published by Praeger (New York) in 1973. Paolo Soleri's work can be seen in the oversize volume, *The City in the Image of Man* (Cambridge, MA: M.I.T. Press, 1970). For a description of what happened when an architect actually built a megastructure, see *Beyond Habitat,* by Moshie Safdie, edited by John Kettle (M.I.T. Press, 1970). My own brief participation in megastructuralism can be found in *The New City: Architecture and Urban Renewal,* a catalogue of an exhibition at the Museum of Modern Art (New York), 1967. See also the evolution of the same megastructure into a more practical proposal in my *Urban Design as Public Policy* (New York: Architectural Record Books, 1974), pp. 156–60.

For a description of megastructures as urban future by someone who at the time was a believer, see Charles Jencks, *Architecture 2000* (New York: Praeger, 1971). For total skepticism on the same subject, see Reyner Banham's *Megastructure: Urban Futures of the Recent Past* (New York: Icon Editions, Harper & Row, 1976). Shadrach Woods' *The Man in the Street* (London: Penguin, 1975) shows how pervasive megastructural thinking briefly became among city designers. Woods, arguing strongly from a humanitarian and individualistic perspective, still accepts megastructural designs as inevitable. For the potential dark side of the megastructural environment, see *Defensible Space: Crime Prevention Through Urban Design,* by Oscar Newman (New York: Macmillan, 1973). For Jane Jacobs' comment on megastructures and large-scale planning in general, see "Vital Little Plans" in *Urban Design International* 2 (January–February 1981).

Index

Picture Credits

1, 2, 3: Illustrations by Karl Gruber from *Ein Deutscher Stadt.*

4: Map of London in 1572 by Frans Hogenberg from Braun and Hogenberg's *Civitates Orbis Terrarum.*

5: Wren's plan in an eighteenth-century engraving reproduced from *The American Vitruvius: An Architect's Handbook of Civic Art,* by Werner Hegemann and Elbert Peets.

6: Sketch by Elbert Peets from *Civic Art.*

7, 8: Engravings from Paul Letarouilly's *Edifces de Rome Moderne.*

9: Drawing by Bartolomeo Neroni from the collection of Donald Oenslager, Morgan Library.

10, 11: Plan and elevation of the Teatro Olimpico from *Civic Art,* by Hegemann and Peets.

12: Photograph of Vatican Library fresco.

13, 14: From *Civic Art,* by Hegemann and Peets.

15: Drawing by Fabrizio Galliari from the collection of Donald Oenslager, Morgan Library.

16: Drawing by Elbert Peets from *Civic Art.*

17: Covent Garden in the eighteenth century, from a contemporary engraving.

18: illustration by Karl Gruber from *Ein Deutscher Stadt.*

19: Andrew Ellicott's engraving as reproduced in *Civic Art,* by Hegemann and Peets.

20: Thomas Jefferson sketch from a manuscript in the Library of Congress, as reproduced in *The City of Man,* by Christopher Tunnard.

21: Drawing by Elbert Peets from the *Journal of the American Institute of Architects,* 1927.

22, 23: Drawings by Elbert Peets from *Civic Art.*

24, 25, 26: Drawings from *Civic Art,* by Hegemann and Peets.

27: Map from *The Art of Town Planning,* by Henry Vaughan Lanchester.

28: Drawing from *Good and Bad Manners in Architecture,* by A. Trystan Edwards.

29: Map from Hegemann and Peets, *Civic Art.*

30: Map from Jean Alphand's *Les Promenades de Paris.*

31: Photograph from *Shepp's Photographs of the World.*

32: Map from Hegemann and Peets, *Civic Art.*

33: From a contemporary photograph.

34: Diagram from *The Art of Town Planning,* by Henry V. Lanchester.

35, 36, 37: From the *Plan of Chicago,* by Daniel H. Burnham and Edward H. Bennett.

38: Map from Hegemann and Peets, *Civic Art.*

39: Map from *The Art of Town Planning,* by Henry V. Lanchester.

40, 41: From *Houses and Gardens of E. L. Lutyens,* by Lawrence Weaver.

42: From *Oppositions 12.*

43, 44, 45, 46: From *Architectural Design.*

47: From *Rob Krier Urban Projects, 1968–1982.*

48, 49: Photos by Laurie Beckleman.

50: Engraving from *London in the Nineteenth Century.*

51: Engraving by Gustave Doré from *London, A Pilgrimmage.*

52, 53: Illustrations by Ebenezer Howard from *Tomorrow: A Peaceful Path to Real Reform.*

54: Engraving of Nash's original design for Regent's Park.

55: Plan of Birkenhead Park from J. Gaudet's *Elements et Theorie de L'Architecture,* vol. 4.

56: Garden plan from *Descriptions Pittoresques de Jardins,* Liepzig, 1802.

57: Photo, Jarrold and Sons, Ltd.

58: Photograph from *The Picturesque,* by Christopher Hussey.

59: Engraving from *Villas and Cottages,* by Calvert Vaux.

60, 61: City College Library.

62–66: From *Town Planning in Practice*, by Raymond Unwin.

67, 68: Map and photo from *Regional Survey of New York and Its Environs*. Vol. 7: *Neighborhood and Community Planning*, published by The Regional Plan Association.

69, 70: From *Neue Baukunst in den Rheinlanden*, by Richard Klapheck.

71, 72: From *Civic Art*, by Hegemann and Peets.

73–76: From *The Housing Book*, by William P. Comstock.

77: From *Neighborhood and Community Planning*.

78–80: From *London Housing*, published by the London County Council in 1937.

81: From *The Building of Satellite Towns*, by C. B. Purdom.

82, 83, 84: From *Neighborhood and Community Planning*.

85: From *City Planning, Housing, A Graphic Review of Civic Art*, vol. 3, by Forester and Weinberg, 1938.

86, 87, 88: From C. B. Purdom's *The Building of Satellite Towns*.

89: Drawing by Robert A. M. Stern Architects.

90: Drawing by Andres Duany and Elizabeth Plater-Zyberk.

91: From *Civic Art*, by Hegemann and Peets.

92: From the first English edition of *Towards a New Architecture*, translated by Frederick Etchells, 1927.

93, 94: From Le Corbusier, *Oeuvre Complete*.

95, 96: From *The Regional Plan of New York and Its Environs*, 1929.

97, 98, 99: From the *Metropolis of Tomorrow*, by Hugh Ferris.

100: Drawing by Tony Garnier from the Etchells translation of Le Corbusier's *Towards a New Architecture*.

101, 102: Photos from *Modern Architecture*, by Bruno Taut.

103, 104: Drawing and model photograph from *Modern Architecture*, catalogue of an exhibition at the Museum of Modern Art, 1932.

105, 107: Drawings from *Dr. H. P. Berlage En Zijn Werk*, 1916.

106: Photograph from *Neue Nederlandische Baukunst*.

108: Photograph from *Modern Architecture*, by Bruno Taut.

109: Photograph by Nory Miller.

110: Photograph from *London Housing*.

111: Photograph from *City Planning, Housing, A Graphic Review of Civic Art*, vol. 3.

112: Diagram from the 1929 *Regional Plan of New York*.

113, 114: Photograph and site plan from *City Planning, Housing, A Graphic Review of Civic Art*.

115: Drawing from Le Corbusier, *Oeuvre Complete*.

116: Photomontage from *A Decade of New Architecture*, by Sigfried Giedion.

117, 118: Photomontages from *Modern Architecture*, by Bruno Taut.

119: Photograph courtesy General Motors.

120: Drawing from the *Greater London Plan*.

121, 122: Drawing from the *County of London Plan*.

123, 124: Photo and drawing from *City Planning in Sweden*, by Kell Astrom.

125: Drawing by Le Corbusier from the *Oeuvre Complete*.

126, 127, 128: City College Library.

129, 130: Photos by the London County Council.

131: Photograph by Chamberlin, Powell and Bon.

132: Model photograph, Victor Gruen Associates.

133: Photograph by Kerry Goelzer.

134: Drawing from a report by the City of Seattle.

135, 136: Drawings from Hegemann and Peet's *Civic Art*.

137, 138: Drawings by Etienne-Louis Boullée from the exhibition catalogue *Visionary Architects*.

139, 140: Victoria & Albert Museum.

141: Drawing from Francisco Mujica's *History of the Skyscraper*.

142, 143: Maps, City College Library.

144, 145: Photomontage and drawing from *Raymond M. Hood*, 1931.

146, 147: Photographs, office of Kenzo Tange.

148: Joseph Molitor photo, courtesy of Paul Rudolph.

149: Model photo, courtesy of Paul Rudolph.

150, 151, 152: From *Archigram 4*.

153: Photomontage from *Archigram*.

154: Drawing by Paolo Soleri from *Paolo Soleri, Projects*.

155: Drawing from *Whitehall: A Plan for the National and Governmental Centre*.

156: Photo by Nory Miller.

Icon Editions